Barcelona Brownsville:
Life in the Hood

Alquan Pinkard

DELANE
PUBLISHING

Copyright © by Alquan Pinkard 2013

ISBN
9780984020478

First Edition: June, 2013

Cover Design and Typesetting by Saforabu Graphix
Cover Photo provided by Alquan Pinkard

Published by Delane Publishing
P.O. Box 195, Wailuku, Maui, HI 96793 USA
Email: books@delanepublishing.com
www.delanepublishing.com

Published in the United States of America

No part of this book may be reproduced or transmitted in any form or by any means, electronic, photocopying, or otherwise, without the express written consent of the publisher.

Printed in USA

Dedication

I dedicate this book to my late grandmother, Virginia Adams, and all my friends that I lost in the streets to senseless violence. I dedicate this book to my grandmother because she was a role model and a big influence on my life. She is one of the reasons I'm still alive today. She tried to keep me out the streets as much as possible, by keeping food in my stomach, money in my pockets and even giving me daily lectures on what can happen to me if I stay in the streets. Without her food, money and advice only the Lord knows where I would be today. I'm also dedicating this book to the friends I lost in the streets, because at any given time they could have been me. Those bullets could have missed them and hit me. I could have not been here today. I am also keeping their memory alive. For all the times we had talks about making it out the hood together. For my Grandmother and the friends I lost, I will strive for success because I know they are watching over me.

Table of Contents

Chapter One: Two Thousand And One … 1

Chapter Two: Summer Fun … 5

Chapter Three: Not As It Seems … 9

Chapter Four: Hood Barbershop … 17

Chapter Five: Project Sports … 21

Chapter Six: Baby Cheaters … 27

Chapter Seven: Inside Hangouts … 33

Chapter Eight: Undercover Brothers … 39

Photo Gallery … 42

Chapter Nine: Hood Boogers Females … 51

Chapter Ten: Family … 55

Chapter Eleven: Gatherings Holidays … 61

Chapter Twelve: Gangs in the Ville … 69

Chapter Thirteen: Gun Play … 81

Chapter Fourteen: Gone But Not 4gotten R.I.P. … 87

Chapter Fifteen: Capital City The Burg … 105

Chapter Sixteen: The Start of the End … 113

Epilogue … 123

Life in the Hood Dictionary … 125

Chapter One: Two Thousand And One

October 31, 2001, seemed like a normal Halloween. Folks were preparing for their Halloween parties for their children. Last minute shoppers were trying to snatch up a costume. Everyone on Pitkin Avenue in Brooklyn, New York, was going trick or treating. I had my Spiderman costume on so anyone I didn't know, you can bet I sprayed them with my web. Spraying folks with my spider web was what actually lead to a big scuffle between the adults that I was with and a group of other passing adults who I'd sprayed. I didn't mean to cause any problems, I just sprayed a man in the New York Sneakers store, next to McDonalds, with my web, and the next thing I hear is, "Y'all Howard niggas better control y'all kids!" No more than five seconds later, I see folks grabbing one another, shoving each other, grappling and tussling, and then I see the cops breaking it up.

When we finally get back to the PJ's everybody laughed about it. Ever since the Twin Towers was taken down by terrorists one month ago in our projects, we couldn't trust no one or anything. And we knew that at any time we could fall prey or become a victim, so when we came home with our Halloween candy our parents became ever more careful. They would check for open candy and throw it away, or the kids would use the candy as a game and throw it at each other.

So it's now around 6pm. The party is in the Howard Housing Projects on the 4th floor, next to building 1550. We're dancing and rocking to Fifty Cent's album, "Power of the Dollar." The place was packed. It seems like hundreds of people were there.

Even Money was at the party eating and carrying on. Money was a bad nigga. He took no shit from no one. He did what he wanted to do, when he wanted to do it, and didn't care about nothing or no one. Everything seemed to be going good. The party was in full swing with the smell of alcohol on people's breath, the smoke of weed hung thick in the air, and the boys in blue being dicks were hanging around. Around 7pm Money leaves the party and said he'll be back shortly.

It is 8pm with no signs of Money. In the hood if you more than thirty minutes late and have not returned, more than likely you're dead or in cuffs. Its 8:45pm now, and the same dicks from before knock on the door and ask for my mother. They show her a picture of Money and ask her if she knows him and his whereabouts. "Why?" My mother replied, "Because around 7:27pm, there was a drug dealer gunned down and he was ID as the shooter," the cops replied. "No I haven't seen him in years" my mother responded, and the cops leave. Later in the night Money returns back to the party, smoking weed and eating food like nothing happened. So I just thought the cops at my door were making a big a mistake, a misunderstanding, if you will.

Weeks later at 5 in the morning, as my family lay sleeping, we are awakened by this loud noise and we hear a big boom at the door. With flash lights shining in our sleepy eyes and guns drawn, the men in blue were shouting, "Get the fuck down or we will shoot." It is the police. They didn't find who they was looking for.

New Year's 2002, the New York Daily News comes out; New York's Top 10 Most Wanted is listed on the front page. Number three is a picture of Money. If you have not guessed it by now, Money is my brother's father. My mother, brother and I goes home around 4 in the morning only to find out the cops had been there, and it was a pad lock on the door. My mother was pissed; we had to go all the way back to my grandmother's house. It was a Saturday so we had to wait until Monday to go to Housing Authority to get the lock off the door.

Winter break is over so it's back to school. I observed many students whispering and pointing at me. They are gossiping and talking about the front page of the New York Daily News with America's Most Wanted and whispering that it's my father who the cops are after. I didn't pay any attention to the students and refused to give them my energy, because that's what people do every day: they gossip. At lunchtime, students were coming up to me saying, "I saw your father in the newspaper." I replied, "That's not my father, and why are you even talking to me?

I don't know you?" All day I was hearing that, and it was beginning to get to me. So the next student that mentioned the negativity to me,

I responded with my own and I gave him a fat lip. This led to a five-day suspension. After the five days were up, I was back in school. Everything seemed back to normal. I didn't see people pointing or whispering. I guess they figured out I wasn't the one to play with.

Chapter Two: Summer Fun

I'm thirteen years old and already know how to ride the trains and buses by myself. I learned how to travel since I was eight years old. You see, I was born and raised in Howard Houses Projects in Brownsville, but I lived in Lafayette Gardens for most of my life. Summer of 2003 was spent in summer school. My behavior in school wasn't acceptable and got me into trouble. I was doing things like, bringing fart bombs to school and throwing them when the teacher wasn't looking. The classroom would be stinking for about ten minutes and then gradually return to normal. I also was making the class laugh by telling jokes about the people in uniforms and the teacher. One time the teacher asked me a question about the lesson we learned. I replied by saying, "Why are you asking me? You're the teacher. I guess you don't know the answer, either." The thing I did regularly was starting paper-ball fights. I would ball up a piece of paper and throw it at whoever wasn't looking. When the teacher asked, "Who did it?" I would point at anyone causing the whole class to begin throwing paper balls.

You know folks are jealous and hating on you when you look good. I remember a lot of the kids were envious and angry at me just because I wasn't from around their way, and because I was a savvy dresser. I always bought the latest gear. I still do. I always had every pair of Jordan's that came out on Saturday. So that Monday I would wear them to school. My mother's model was that you can't have a new pair of sneakers without at least two new outfits. So if I wasn't wearing Coogi, I would have on Roca Wear or Sean John. Every day she would give me five dollars to go to school with. So while everybody was drinking milk or water, I would laugh because I was buying soda or juice. Folks would try to do stupid stuff, just to irritate me enough to piss me off by stepping on my foot to dirty up my sneakers. And this would eventually lead to me losing my cool and knocking some heads by fighting. The fighting led me to the principal's office, and the principal dished out the punishment of suspension, which led to my grades suffering, which led me to being in summer school with 100 degree hot weather. Dang! Thirty-five days of summer school, and no kids said or did nothing stupid. Not one of them tried to step on my sneakers. I found it very surprising. I guess they were smart enough not to want to repeat the same grade over by creating trouble. No one threatened to spill milk on my shirt. Since I was kind of the class clown, students would make noises and said I did it. I usually would get in trouble for it, but this summer school, that didn't even happen. When the final three days of school remained, that's when everything changed. I'll never forget it. I remember it clearly, like it was yesterday. I was in the bathroom, and four boys came into the bathroom and challenged me by saying, "Who you think you are?" Now, I never back down to anyone, and me being the person that I am, I said "For sure nothing like you punks." I'm surrounded by four kids and the next thing I know I'm on the floor with one sneaker on. I finally managed to get to my feet and make my way out into the hallway to get my other sneaker. The boys started playing monkey in the middle, tossing my sneaker around to one another while I was the one in the middle. This was pissing me off, and I was getting mad, but I maintained my cool, but kept a smirk on my face. Of course I got my sneaker back, but I made sure they knew nothing of how I hid my anger. I can always maintain a cool interior, even though I may be burning up inside. I always thought, never lose your cool, you can win at any situation. My turn will come, I'll get them back, and this is what I did.

    The next day after school I was walking to my home in Lafayette Gardens and I see a crowd of boys, so I made a detour in the store. The crowd of boys followed me in the store and grabbed my book bag, and I punched the person closest to me. They all jumped on me.

    On the last day of school, it is a half day and when you're told that you've passed and completed summer school, you can leave early. Everyone was laughing when I walked by because of what happened in the store the other day with the boys ganging up on me. All the kids were leaving school, and just as soon as they open the front door to leave the school, there were at least fifty of my peeps waiting outside that door. The school kids didn't know who they were, but I sure did. Next, I just watched all the kids exiting the school doors. Then I saw all of the boys that ganged up on me in the store, and if they had looked at me wrong, I would point at them and you can use your imagination here and guess what happened next. After they got their beat down, we begin to leave the school area, smiles on our faces and screaming to the top of our lungs, "BROWNSVILLE, NEVER RAN, NEVER WILL." School safety officers came out and began chasing us. We dashed off and ran to the train station and hopped over the turn-style without paying our fare. Our attitudes and thoughts were, "Shucks, what we look like paying our fare, and it's fifty of us strong?"

Just as we pulled into Broadway Junction Station, the power on the train cut off. We saw a lot of flashing lights and thought the police was there to arrest us for not paying our fare. I pulled the door open and we all ran, not knowing the whole city was out of power. BLACK OUT! By the time we got to the hood we saw everyone was hanging outside, and the Johnny Pump was on full blast since there was no air conditioning on. Folks were keeping cool by hosing down with the Johnny Pump on. It was a madhouse everywhere with the lights out, especially in the hood. Everyone was running around like a chicken with its head chopped off. All the stores were rushing to close up their doors early to avoid robberies. The thugs and hoodlums were out in full gear getting theirs, and the little cops was scared, but they were out too.

By 7pm, it began to get dark so I decide to be an arsonist for the day and set the garbage can on fire to give us some light in the park. Then we got the light that we didn't want to see; blue and white police lights. Shortly after we don't see anyone, but we hear footsteps and following the footsteps, there were at least two dozen gun shots ringing in the hot muggy air. I heard bullets whistling pass me and hitting the handball court, so I drop to the ground. Then I seen someone run by and throw a gun in the garbage. After all the gun shots stopped, I get up quickly and tried to run to my building, soon

I was being tackled by a Police Officer because he thought I was a suspect. He asked if I had seen anyone run this way, I said, "No", and the Po Po let me go and told me it's not safe to be out here. I run to my building. Throughout the night we hear numerous rounds of gun shots and screams. Too many for me to count or tell you if the screams were cries of someone being hit or screams of people who was in shock. I just couldn't tell you.

It was too hot to sleep in the house, so everyone was outside sleeping on the benches, and since there was no power to cook and eat, folks pulled out their grills and begin to BBQ. We are between the ages of thirteen and sixteen years old and trying to grill. Amber pretended that she knew what she was doing and thought she was a cook. Amber put the lighter fluid in the grill and lit it and closed the lid. About two minutes later she lifts the lid up to see if the fire was still going. All I heard was a swoosh noise as the fire burst out and her side burns caught on fire. Once I knew she was all right I burst out laughing. I couldn't breathe after a while from my guts busting. I finally control myself to get close enough to see her side burns had turned into gray ash. Out of nowhere I heard someone say, "She got a gray face." I tried to hold my laughter in but I couldn't. Amber burst into tears, which made everyone laugh harder. We stayed up all night and laughed about Amber's gray ash and the swooshing sound the grill made.

As the sun rises the next morning, everyone goes in their house to do whatever it is that they do. I go take a shower and then off to my bed. As I'm sleeping I hear the air conditioner come on. I jumped and I screamed out the window at the top of my lungs, "WE HAVE POWER EVERYBODY!"

Chapter Three: Not As It Seems

Everything wasn't always good as it seemed. Once I got to high school, everything changed. I was going to South Shore High School in the day time and the PAL gym at night. For the first couple weeks of school, I never went to my last period and I always came to school third period. The first month of high school, I had a fight with a boy from Compton because I told him he was on the East Coast now. All that gang shit and acting tough was out the window. That led to a suspension, which led to my mother finding out I barely been going to school. So she took me out of the PAL basketball program. When I finally went back to school, I went to all my classes only because I met a girl in first and eighth period. She was a light-skin, thick girl from the Pink Houses Project. That year I even failed gym, so I know it was going to be a long high school career for me. The last day of freshman year, I received my last report card and only had one credit. So when I went back to Howard, there's a cookout on the hill and it's packed. So a lady was just sitting on the bench. Then she finally asked for food, and they gave her a frank. A couple minutes later she must have slid off cause nobody saw her. Just when I'm about to go tell my mother a lie about my report card, at least fifteen unmarked police cars pulled up. The same lady that asked for a frank was an undercover cop and was the first officer to make an arrest.

All the older people that were holding the hood down were now in jail. So that whole summer, people from other projects was coming to the hood shooting it up, and no one was doing anything to stop them. So the up-and-coming had no one to look up to, so they went out and bought their own weapons. Mostly lil kids between the age of fourteen and sixteen, from the other projects came around the next day and shot up the hood again, no one did anything. Then an older nigga in the hood walked up to us and said, "You all soft. They would have never been doing that when I was your age." So everyone looked at each other and said, "Go get the grip: we about to turn it up." Around 1 am, three boys under the age of sixteen went to the other projects and shot it up, and one person from the other projects got hit in an artery and almost died. After that night, every black male teenager under the age of sixteen, their lives were changed forever, even if they had nothing to do with it, just cause they was from Howard. I would walk around, and older dudes would either say "Y'all should of killed him, that's wassup, what y'all did" or, "I hope you got your grip on you because they're going to come back blazing." Since I was from Howard and many in Brooklyn did not like our hood, I had to protect myself.

We ganged up the next couple of weeks and put money in a box so we can purchase our own weapons instead of asking people to borrow their weapons. We use to sit on the rooftop all day and night with chirps and let everybody know what we were watching. That year the coaches ended the basketball tournament because they didn't want to be responsible for anybody's death. The summer of Two-thousand-six, we witnessed shooting every day, but no one was shot, so the cops never did show their face around our hood. The next two years were just about the same. Two-thousand and seven and two thousand and eight came, and then everything got critical over a basketball game. Van Dyke projects vs. Howard houses were playing the championship game. Van Dyke was losing by at least 15 points with less than ninety seconds to go. So a Van Dyke player named David was hard fouling the other team, and that lead to everyone going wild, including the fans on the sidelines who were outraged. Then I saw David get subbed out the game, and someone on the sideline gave him a bag, so I told Chesse, who is a gangsta from Howard, to watch him. Then Chesse tapped Bricks, who is also a gangsta from Howard. Then the two of them went on opposite sides of the park and watched everybody that was not from Howard. When the game was over, David went on the side of the park and started shooting in the air, and everybody was falling, I thought they were getting shot. Then I looked at Chesse and Bricks, and they both started shooting at David at the same time. Since my building was close by, Chesse ran to my house, and when we got up there my grandmother was praying, so we put the gun in the closet and went back outside before she finished. As we stepped out the elevator we were greeted by two people from Howard with guns and asked, "Was y'all shooting at them Glenmore niggas?" Then one of them said, "I knew we should have clipped David when he was on the bike." We all walked to the back of the hood, and most of the 73rd precinct was out there picking up bullet cases and looking at the cars with bullet holes in them. As we looked up towards the other projects, we saw David and a group of people walking towards our projects. But when they saw the cops they all turned back around. We all looked at each other and said, "It's real now, nobody get caught slipping."

The next day at the tournament no one from the opposing team played in the game. However they came on bikes to scope the scene out. There were cops on duty in the park to make sure nothing happened. That night when we were chilling, somebody called Chesse phone and said it's like ten people near the store. That night Jason happens to be with us while he was home visiting on college vacation. As we walked towards the store in different directions, Jason stayed on the bench. By the time we got near the library I'm the only person that seen people ducking behind cars. I told everyone to look, and as they paused to look, David and his crew jumped from behind the cars and started shooting. My crew started back paddling and shooting back. We ran towards the back of the hood in the direction of 30 and 40 Glenmore Avenue. As we were running I see Jason flying as if he is an Olympic track star running the one hundred meter dash. I clocked him at twelve seconds. That's how fast he was running. He was mad dashing towards his house. The shooting stopped for a split second and we started walking. Then it started again. As I raised my hand to shoot back, I felt something brush against my hand and saw Johnson stumble, saying that he got hit. By the time I got to the building, I see Jason on the roof of his house screaming "ARE YALL GOOD?!" I'm thinking, "Like nigga, we almost died, so what you think?" We are all in the spot and my wrist is bleeding. It seems as if I got grazed by the bullet that hit Johnson. Other than that we are all good, and our blood is running with adrenaline. We are freaking hyped and talking about what happened and how nobody got hit. After twenty minutes, we head back outside, this time we only carry one gun with us. We stashed our gun when we saw the Po Po driving through. As they pass leaving the hood, it was as if nothing happened. As everybody was carrying on outside, we see two people flying past, and they said they saw two people on bikes with hoodies coming from Gee's. We started stumbling when we saw the bike turn the corner because it was unexpected. Everyone was trying to run instead of going for the gun that was right next to us. David jumped off the bike shooting, while chasing after us. Everyone was falling over each other. I hear bullets whistling by my ear and over my head, and hitting the building.

Somebody was smart enough to get the gun and start shooting back, and that was enough to make David and his boy run in the opposite way. Now we are on the hill chilling recounting what just happened and realize we are pissed off. We are standing there and Chesse shows us he has a hole in his shirt and that he was bleeding on his side. Luckily he only got grazed. The next day I go to Jason's house and his mother said, "Is that you out there shooting like a wild animal?" As I was about to answer her, she says, "I'm just messing with you."

Since Jason was never in trouble and no one knew him, we kept some of our weapons at his house. That night everything was going good. There was no shooting and no cops harassing us. Then Jason said, "Let me just shoot it in the air to see how it feels." Just as I was going to get the gun for him to shoot, the D's pulled up. I said, "See you lucky. You would of been on your way to the tombs." We laughed, and he replied, "Ain't no way they would have caught me. I would have been too scared. I would have jumped over the gate, threw the gun and been in my window before they would have got out the car." Everybody started die laughing, and the D's pulled up and said, "What the fuck y'all laughing for? It's either we going to arrest y'all or we going to let them kill y'all, cause we tired of this shooting shit." Then I said, "Y'all have to catch us first", and just as they started opening their doors, we ran.

That same night around 2am we were outside having fun. Then

Bricks said, "Let's go have fun over at their projects." We got our weapons. Some were hidden in stashes. Others had their girls carry them in their pocketbooks. When we reached the other projects parking lot my cousin asked me to wait because Cindy was over there. I acted like we were going to wait as she was calling Cindy. At least fifty gun shots were let off. Cindy came back to the hood saying that we were lucky that she didn't get hit. And we said, "You're lucky you didn't get hit."

The next night we were outside drinking, smoking, rolling dice, and having fun. Next an argument started about who got more money and hoes. Then a fight started after Chesse said, "I bet I can hit it with your mother if I wanted to." It ended fast once a fiend came up to the crowd and said, "I got this for sale." I thought he was going to pull out a phone or iPod or something. This nigga pulled out a 9mm and said he want ten bags for it. We started arguing again about who was going to give him the ten bags. This dope fiend got the nerve to say, "Since y'all fighting, I'll sell it to them other niggas." It got so quiet you could hear a pin drop. I said, "If you even leave from in front of this building, we will beat the crack out of you." Then Chesse and I gave him five bags each. Next we went up to the roof to test the gun out to make sure that it worked. Chesse was only supposed to fire two shots in the air to make sure that it worked, but he let the whole clip go. We got so hype, we starting shooting all the guns in the air, wasting bullets but at the same time having fun. Some of my crew from the other side of the hood would call my phone and ask, "Son, did they come through," and I would say, "We got new toys on deck." We were running out of bullets and guns due to people getting chased and tossing them. I started selling weed to get money for guns, bullets, and clothes since that's what the females liked.

Nothing's been happening for a couple of days. Then Johnson called my phone and said for me to meet him by the park. I get to the park and I see everybody we got beef with and I'm thinking, "Wtf was he doing, trying to set me up?" Then I see Chesse and Bricks sitting on the bench and when I get up to them, they say, "These niggas trying to dead the beef, but we gripped if they try some funny shit." I get to

Johnson and the people we got beef with and I hear them say, "We beefing over nothing, we shooting everyday and no fiends coming, so we not getting money." So those niggas shook hands and walked off, but I can tell the beef wasn't over. Chesse said he was leaving for the night and that he would see me in the morning. Then he gave me eight dollars for a ten dollar bag of weed. Since he was my man I gave it to him. He then asked me to switch guns with him because he had a .45 caliber and I had a quarter water. He didn't want to walk up the hill with a big gun. The next morning a girl from the hood that I had sex with before was at my door around 8am and said, "David is in front of 30." So I told her to hold the gun and we went outside. When we turned the corner there were two blue and white officers standing there looking at me, so I thought they knew something. I started fumbling, and my weed fell out my pants leg, and the officers saw it. By time I picked it up, they were already walking towards me, so I ran. They chased me in the building, and I ran up the stairs. I knew they would stop because they were scared to chase a black kid in the exit due to a cop killing earlier that year. In the process they ran past the girl with the gun. She called me and asked me what to do with the gun. I told her to take it to Jason's house. I changed my clothes and came out around 11am and saw the same cops that chased me. They stopped me and frisked me and then asked me why did I run? I replied, "Why did yall chase me?" Then I walked off.

    I got to Bricks and asked him did he see Chesse? He said Chesse just called and said he is on his way. Around 2pm we were all chilling when Chesse's older brother pulled me to the side and said, "Chesse just got shot and they got him cuffed to the bed." I didn't tell anyone, yet they knew something was bothering me. Later that night everyone was asking me if Chesse got shot? I would say, "I didn't hear that." His older brother came to me again around midnight and said,"You ready to make a movie?" I didn't say anything. We just started walking towards Glenmore. As we get into Glenmore we don't see anybody, and that seemed strange, so I started looking around and saw a group of people walking towards the store. So when they came back from the store we jumped out from behind the wall and chased them for a couple of yards and started squeezing. By time we get back to the hood, we see the ambulance pull up to Glenmore. Two people from Glenmore were hit but they lived to tell everybody that bullets burn. I go to my house, and I hear my grandmother praying on her knees to God that I don't die in these streets. She heard me come in. I toss the gun in the closet before she sees it, she asks, "What's going on?" I tell her, "People were shooting in the air, that's all." I would try to leave and she would ask me where was I going? And I would tell her that I was going upstairs to my friend's house, and she would always say to me to be careful. That night I get on MySpace and I have at least a dozen messages from people from Glenmore and Van Dyke Projects who said that they were going to kill us. I paid them no mind, but the next couple of days they would come to the hood shooting at anyone they saw. So as we all were in front of 40 planning on how we was going to corner them, the same D's from before came and said they are tired of this shit and told us to go in the building. They let one of us go because he was twelve years old. I'm guessing while we were in the building somebody from the 40 told the cops where the gun was at, because they came back and said, "We told you we would get you." Next they showed us the gun they found. Not knowing there were four other guns stashed away, they locked us up. Once the cuffs went on my wrist I knew it was real. We get to the 73rd, and I call Chesse's brother and tell him what happened, and this nigga said, "I just saw yall, so stop lying 'cause I'm trying to get some head." The entire sixty hours that we spent in the 73rd precinct, the cops interrogated us, and they were making up lies, saying things like, "Your boy said it was yours so you better tell us the truth." Every time one of us got questioned I heard our boys laughing so hard, and I knew by their laughter no one was telling the cops anything. We looked up and saw someone from Glenmore in cuffs and we all started screaming "PUT HIM IN THIS CELL" That was the last time we would see him, so I'm guessing he gave up information and they let him go. Finally the van to Central Booking came and we sat in C.B. for another thirty hours before seeing the judge. Being that they didn't find the gun on none of us, all of us were released except for the two people that had warrants for not paying fines.

    We got to the hood to see if the other guns were there, and they were gone. We were told that one of our boys came and took them after we got locked up. When we came home, it was Howard Day so everyone in Howard was having a cook out. As I walked in the building my Grandmother said, "What are you doing carrying guns?" I told her, "Grandma, they lied. They just locked us up for nothing." I got in the house to take a shower 'cause I was stink, hungry and felt sick. We all came back out at the same time and we hit up every cook out in the hood. Next, we see the other two people hours later as they were just coming home. We greeted them with our usual high fives, and Bricks said, "Yo, yall niggas smell like yall washed up in that milk they gave us in Central Bookings." We started bugging out laughing. At that point, I literally had tears in my eyes. That was the end of the shootings for a while. A couple of months later, Chesse comes home and tell us the story about how he got shot leaving Cindy's house.

Chapter Four: Hood Barbershop

Who needed a barber shop when we had a hood barber? Junior the barber lived in my grandmother's building, so our parents never had to worry about us crossing the streets, the crazy drunk drivers swerving, a kid getting killed by a hit-and-run driver, getting shot or robbed because we were from Howard. When I was young, our parents treated Junior the Barber's crib like it was a day care center.

They would bring all the kids to Junior the barber, leave us and come back hours later. Since Junior was known by my mother, and cool with her, she gave him permission to hit me if I moved. I hated that. Every time Junior would begin to cut my hair I would move my head, and he would pluck me in my forehead and say, "Stop moving." I would cry and start kicking my feet. The thing I loved about going to get a haircut is that you can do so many fun things there. While waiting, you could play Sega or Nintendo games. I use to always play Mortal Combat or Street Fighter.

Junior the Barber even had boxing gloves so we would box each other. One thing that I loved is that in the middle of the living room it actually was a skelly court. So the hallway always stayed dirty and sticky because the kids would buy the pushup ice cream that had the Flintstones on it, in order to get the top. It was kind of fun to get a haircut if you think about it. I used to have so much fun that I would go there when I didn't need a haircut, just to play the games. It was always crowded, so people were coming just too chill out, which made it crazy packed in the house. You would always hear someone complaining because a kid that was playing Skelly was blocking the view of the TV, or somebody playing the game kicked another person's Skelly top. Those were the good old days.

Nowadays we got the same barber, just a different location. Now we have to cross the streets and watch for cars and crazy drunk drivers. It's the same fun but it's dangerous now if you get caught getting a hair cut at the wrong time. It could end up being your last hair cut. Man!

They even up their items and game systems in the shop. The barber shop has a 50-inch TV where folks gamble and bet their money on fights and sports. There is a mini diner/store in the barber shop.

While you are waiting or watching TV, you can order hot or cold food. Every once in a while, somebody would bring in hot wings or french fries back and say, "Yo, it got hair in it." And someone else would respond, "Hello! This is a barber shop, what do you expect?" You don't need to go out and get anything to eat because the mini store was there. You would hear all the latest gossip and what's happening in the hood or you could talk about anything in the barber shop as long as no ladies were around. I would hear people talk about how fat a lady's ass was and what they would do to it. Then it's always that one person, who would come in and say, "Oh I hit that already, it wasn't all that." If you wanted to know who got their ass whip or shot the night before, the barber shop was the place to get your news. You could get a haircut and get the hood news at the same time. But if you were doing your own little thing on the side, the shop was a good place to be. We still can go to the barber shop and play games while we wait.

If you had a good hustle such as a CD or a book, they would let you sell your product out of the barber shop. The shop is the place where you can hustle just about anything. They would host a one-on-one tourney for people 30 years and older. If you guess forty-one out of fifty winners you can win $100. The catch was you had to pay $5 to place your bet. Nobody ever guesses forty-one right, so they would always make a lot of money off that. Besides the shop, we had the bodega that sold everything the shop didn't. If we hold them down, they would hold us down. People would try to rob the owner when he would walk through the hood to go buy weed. A couple of times, either the young shooters saved him or the older dealers saved him. In pay back, he would tell us there is a secret room in the back where we can hide if the police ever chased us. Sure enough, everybody that was near the store and got chased hid in that secret room. I remember one time I was in the store when a drug dealer ran in and threw his gun to the owner and ran back out. He got caught, but had no weapons on him, so the police had to let him go. Louie, the owner of the bodega, started bringing guns from his country and selling them for next to nothing. Police were scared to come to the hood once they started hearing K's go off. Shortly after that, Louie started selling liquor in the store. Since Louie was opened 24 hours and the liquor store closed early, folks would buy a bottle from Louie even though it cost $10 more than the liquor store. I guess selling heroes and sodas wasn't enough for them: they needed to sell something stronger. Next thing we know, every store in the hood started to sell liquor. That didn't last long because the cops started to raid all the stores shortly thereafter. One of the stores on East New York Avenue was thirsty to be down.

    This store gave a scam artist $10,000 to pay all their bills for the next month and were force to close their doors because they didn't have any money. That's why it pays to be original. Every store went downhill, except Louie's store. Still to this day Louie continues to make the best hero sandwiches. The pool store, across the street from the pool, thought they were keeping up because everybody from little kids to crack heads, drug addicts and dope fiends would chill in the back store. They were so busy trying to keep up they forgot how to run the store. Nobody was buying anything from their store. We would go there just to chill. And when people did buy product, they would always be short of cash, so the store wasn't making any money. Once again another store couldn't keep up so they were forced to close their doors. This is life in the hood.

Chapter Five: Project Sports

Growing up, kickball was like a national sport for us in the Ville. From the streets to the school yard, kickball was the sport every kid wanted to play. I only say the Ville because when I would chill in Bedford Stuyvesant, no one wanted to play kickball. Most were interested in basketball. We had our own stomping ground for kick ball in the hood. Between 30 and 40 was the field. It wasn't really a field, but that's where everything went down. All the kids would come to 30 and 40 to play hood sports: from kickball to Skelly or hopscotch to jump rope. Mostly kickball, though. We would basically bully everyone because it was more people playing kickball rather than anything else. We needed more room to play. Older folks would sit on the bench to enjoy the laughter of us kids. They wouldn't admit it, yet we secretly knew that they hated us to play kickball because we couldn't control the direction the ball went in. So most times we would leave them ducking or putting their hands up for cover. One time I was up to kick the ball when Rakim rolled the ball. I know you thinking, like, WTF is a nigga name Rakim doing in the hood? We now call him Doughboy for specific reasons. Like I said, Doughboy rolled the ball and I ran so fast to kick the ball that I put all my leg strength into it. As my left leg began to rise I watched the ball roll past. As the ball passed, I felt my right leg leaving the ground. Suspended in mid-air, I was going down fast. That was my first time I really looked up at the sky. As I was getting up from the ground, I hear nothing but laughter and people rolling on the ground from cracking up. I finally get up and check myself. I see a big dirt stain on my back from the ground, so you know I was mad with everyone laughing at me. And that didn't help matters. Doughboy started screaming, "You out, you don't even get three chances because you fell that hard." I told him to shut up and roll the ball. This time I kicked the ball so hard I thought it was going to hit the building. Instead it hit Ms. Hardy in her head, and her grandson Blue, caught the ball, and I was out. Everyone went to make sure Ms. Hardy was all right, she said she was okay long as I was out. I was the only one smirking because I thought seeing an old person's head bounce of a ball was funny. I played the outfield when we were down, so I can just let my chuckles out. As I was laughing I didn't realize Bricks had kicked the ball and it was coming in my direction. By the time I noticed it, the ball already had fallen directly in front of me, which led to the other team winning.

Kickball wasn't the only sport we played, just one of the biggest. We had stomping grounds for every sport we played in different sections of the hood. We had two places where we played football because we played tackle or two-hand touch. We played two-hand touch in the parking lot by the rent office. There would be people from the soft side of Howard already in the parking lot. We called it the soft side because there was almost no crime on that side of the projects. People from the rent office building would also be there, so that would be their team. Our team was people from the hill and 30 and 40. Everyone except for Blue, was the only nigga in the hood that couldn't leave in front of 30 or 40 without his mom. Nowadays, Blue is seen running around wild, his mom and grandma don't know, so they still think he's good old Blue. Because Blue can never play, we were always one player short, and since the other team didn't want to sit nobody out, we had to play like that. You would think we would lose every game because of that, but actually we won like ninety percent of the games we played. Once we started playing in the circle, our percentage drop just a little. Blue's mother can see him from the circle, but he never wanted to play because it was tackle, so we were still one man short. That made it hard for us to win. The best player on our team was Yellowman, and that made it easy to put two people on him.

Daquan was the quarterback and he thought Yellowman was so good he was still trying to pass him the ball. That would come back to actually bite Yellowman in his ass. Daquan drew up a play for Yellowman to go deep for a Hail Mary pass. He tossed the ball as far as he could and Yellowman had his man beat or so he thought.

Just as Yellowman reached for the ball, he was blindsided by Eric. We could tell by the impact that it was going to be an ugly scene. When Eric got up his mouth was bleeding and he was missing a tooth. When Yellowman got up from the ground, his forehead was bleeding, and Eric's tooth was stuck in his forehead. Once he took the tooth out, he started leaking a lot of blood. I ran and got his grandmother, and she pressed a wet towel on his forehead, and then we waited for the ambulance to come. When the ambulance finally arrived on the scene they were taking their slow time walking to us, like we were not important in the hood. The paramedics told Yellowman to remove the wet towel. When he did, blood dripped down the side of his face. Yellowman asked, "Am I'm going to need stitches?" They did not respond to him. The paramedics asked his grandmother if she wanted them to stitch him up in the ambulance to save a trip to the hospital. Once Yellowman heard that he took off running. He cleared and jumped over the first high gate in his path. His grandmother shook her head and said, "$10 to whoever catch him and hold him." Both teams took off running after him. Shortly thereafter, at least five folks were holding him on the ground. After he got his stitches he was scared to do anything. If the wind blew too hard, he would cry saying his forehead hurt. Some tough guy he was! That was the last time we played football in the circle.

Stomping grounds for Baseball were in the path on the hill. We called it "The Path" because it had a path on each side. Yellowman had everything we needed to play baseball. He even had a left hand glove for me. Yellowman and I were never on the same team when we played baseball. Teams really didn't matter because there was always room for another person. We made sure we played with a softball because people would get hit in the face and the ball would always hit windows. If it was a hardball, we would have death and broken windows on our hands. And the way I was smacking that ball when I was at bat, I didn't want death on my conscience. One game I was on fire. I didn't even know I could do what I was doing. I was hitting doubles and triples all game, then I hit a home run, and the ball went in the street and we couldn't find it. This meant that now I had to run to the store on Thatford Avenue to get another ball. After I came back from the store, we continued the game, and my team was down by one run in the 5th inning. In the hood, we're not playing nine-innings games. Five-innings was the most we would play. It was two outs and Hammer was up before me. He hit a line drive and made it to the tree. The tree was first base. I was up at bat, and the ball was pitched. I pointed to the street as if I was going to hit it that far. I swung the bat very hard and it connected with the ball. I ran with my head down, and as I looked up to see where Hammer was, I heard a loud noise like a little gun went off. Then I seen the ball fly in the air and Hammer falling to the ground. Next thing I hear is Yellowman screaming, "We won! We won! Since the ball hit Hammer, he was automatically out. Yellowman didn't give a flying fuck that Hammer could be hurt, and they lived next door to each other for as long as I can remember. He was just glad that his team won. Talk about sportsmanship! Luckily, Hammer was okay. He had a nice size lump his on head where the ball had hit him.

Basketball was the same thing. The big park on a nice sunny day was our stomping grounds for basketball. It was crowded. There were a total of seven courts that you can play on. But if you were playing on the two middle courts, you were nice. Nice meaning you were very good at playing and you were worth playing against good competition. To get on the court you had to come out bright and early and claim your spot. I remember when I was sent to the store around 9am by my grandmother to get her coffee and a newspaper. I would walk by the park to see who was on the court, and if people were balling, you can bet she wouldn't get her coffee and newspaper until noon, around 2pm if my team kept winning. And you can bet around those times I would have that belt on my ass for not coming right back. Garbage players would be outside early just to call next, so when the good players come out and ask who got next, they say them. The garbage players get happy when the good players say I'm running with you. It was one Rican nigga name Nelson that thought he was so nice when he was trash. I actually think he is mentally retarded. He can make a few open shots and thought he had a crazy crossover that can make anybody fall. It was funny because I always had to guard him. Yellowman and I were always on the same team. I hated it because Nelson would run around the whole game and don't get the ball, and I would get tired. So when I wouldn't chase Nelson, he would be open and score. Yellowman got loud and said, "Why is he scoring? If he scores again I'm holding his retarded ass." He didn't score again. To top it off, I hit the game winning three pointer. So Nelson and his team were off the court and we started screaming next. Snotty and Bricks had next. These two niggas think that they are the best duo in the world. Snotty wanted to dribble all day cause' he had a lil handle, and Bricks wanted to shoot all day cause' he had a lil jumper. Bricks was always short so I would punch his ball when he shot. As we were playing, we see Nelson sitting on top of the hoop on another court. Then he tries to stand up. You know nothing good can come from this. Nelson stands up and jumps through the hoop and then grabs the rim by hanging down. He starts bouncing up and down like a monkey. So Snotty starts throwing the ball at him, and Nelson said that don't hurt. He throws the ball one last time, and you see Nelson start to fall. I'm thinking he is going to land on his feet. That nigga fell head first. Soon as he hit the hard concrete ground, blood spurted everywhere. Snotty took off running. Before we knew it, he was by 48 and in his building. When Nelson got up from the ground, it looked like a movie because his face was mad bloody and he started screaming. He had to get over a hundred stitches and go to therapy because his speech was slurred. Once again Yellowman got to say something. He said, "Not to be funny, but didn't Nelson look like that bloody scream mask when he got up?" Everyone started laughing so hard. This is my story how I came up in the hood on all sports. We always had fun, but dumb shit is bound to happen when you're playing sports in the hood.

Chapter Six: Baby Cheaters

Party! Party! Party! Let's all get wasted! Hood parties were the best. If you were in Brooklyn, then you knew about Baby Cheaters. This is what we called our party spot. We had the best parties ever. We had people from all over New York come in Baby Cheaters to have a good time. There would be folks all the way from Coney Island that would party there. At first it just was suppose to be for people from the hood, but then somehow word started getting out that this was the best place to party. Next thing we know it was lines of people waiting to get into our parties. After a while they started charging everybody to get in, and would use that money for rent because we know the person who lived in that crib didn't have a job. The parties were so popping we figure why not have one every day of the summer? And sure enough that's what we did.

Every day the whole hood was ghost town until you hit the front of building 48, then you see hundreds of folks and you hear Sean Paul song, Get Busy playing. My boy Darius lived in the same building, so we would always chill at his house until it was party time. Even if it wasn't a party we would be at his house anyway, just chilling. Everyone smokes and drinks with the exception of me. So while everybody was in the back of the house drinking and smoking I would be in the front of the house with Darius parents, playing Xbox. Every time that good old Sunday dinner was done I was always getting the first plate. By the time everyone in the back realized the food was done, it would almost be gone. I use to play Darius step-father in 2k basketball game for money and I always use to win. So he use to change the rules saying "Let's play like this; whoever is winning after each quarter gets paid, and whoever wins the whole game gets double the money." He would be winning after most quarters, but I would win the game, so no one would win or lose money that way. I told him that was a smart way for him not to lose money or look like a sore loser. There was a spot on his floor where all the drug dealers and smuts would stay at. So every time when we leave Darius house to go outside there would be dope fiends in the hallway or even the police peeking out of the exits. There were plenty of times when the police made us go back in the house so they can stake out the neighbor's apartment. Not knowing we already called the dealers and let them know the cops was out there. So by the time the cops raided the house all the drugs was either out the window or flushed.

A couple of days went by, and I was coming out of Darius house. Yellowman, Darius, and I were making noise in the hallway, and the drug dealers came out in the hallway and told me to come inside. In my mind I was thinking why they wanted me to come in? I went in anyway. Once I was in one of the dealers asked did I want any liquor or weed, and I said, "No." Then he asked, "Do you have a condom?" I was thinking like, "Nigga I aint gay!"

Then another dealer said, "Nah, he ain't fucking. Just let the lil nigga get some head."

I went in the back room with one of the drug dealers, and there was a half-naked woman lying down, asleep. The dealer then slapped the girl's ass and said, "Wake up! I got a job for you. Give my lil man some head" She replied, "No, I'm not going to go to jail. He is a little boy."

The drug dealer said, "I bet when he pull down his pants he won't be a little boy if you do your job right." She asked, "How old are you?" I told her that I was fourteen. She said, "OMG! I'm going to go to jail! Hurry up and pull ya pants down." I was horny once I pulled my pants down. Then the drug dealer came back in the room and said, "Make sure you use lip gloss on my son." Once he came back in the room, I wasn't horny any more.

She asked me was I ready and I told her no. After that she said, "You better use your hand then." Once I was ready, that was the best feeling in the world. That was my first time getting head, and it was by a grown ass woman. I didn't know what was going on but I know it felt good and she said, "Don't look at me while I'm giving you head."

I thought to myself, as if I was going to listen to her. Just as she put her head back, I had this funny feeling in my stomach and I couldn't really talk. Then the next thing I hear her screaming, "WTF you got it all over the room you better clean this shit up!" She went in the bathroom to do whatever.

Not long after, the drug dealers said, "Damn! I forgot you were here. Was the head good?" I just put two thumbs up and walked into the bathroom, as she was walking out. When I finished cleaning myself up., I heard them tell the girl to go brush her teeth so that she could roll weed. When I was leaving the apartment, the dealers said, "You our little man and don't ever say we didn't do anything for you." I walked back in the hallway and Darius was still there with Yellowman. They started laughing and said, "Damn she got you cheesing and sweating." Remind you, it was the middle of winter, and it was freezing, but I was sweating, so you know it had to be good. The next day, all the drug dealers from the hood would come up to me and say, "Now you the man! I heard what happen last night."

Man! When I was younger, all we did was party and have good times. We use to party on the soft side. The soft side of the hood was a place where there was a bunch of nobodies who gave parties to fit in. The nobodies were hoping that by throwing these parties, they could be cool with everyone in hood. We would always see them around but wouldn't say anything to them. So one weekend, they gave a party and it was popping.

I didn't know the hood had so many girls in it. I guess the freaks really do come out at night. So the party was in full effect. It was crowded and everyone was dancing, we were chilling, and the smuts were acting wild. Then an argument between Yellowman and a girl breaks out but it was quickly stopped. I told him to come with me to the chicken spot, but he didn't want to go, so I went by myself. When I got back from the chicken spot before I turn the corner to get to the hood, I hear a lot of noise. I finally see everybody that was at the party pouring out of the building and I see Yellowman with his shirt off. He came up to me and said, "Son these niggas pussy let me get jumped." First thing I said was, "Where they at? Let's violate them." Next he told me he got jumped by three girls. I couldn't stop from laughing. He told me the girls were slapping him in his face and he knocked one of them out. The entire time he was telling me the story, I was laughing and the girls that jumped him looked good, very pretty, so that made it even funnier.

The next day was Baby Cheaters again and for some reason there were more people than the night before. I figure something was going to pop off because when there's a lot of black people in one place, nothing good can come from it. We were partying when the music stopped abruptly, and the next thing I see was pushing and shoving. Everybody ran out the house because Lore and Lucas was going at it. They were two of most dangerous people in the hood at the time. The crowd poured outside and we see Lore spit in Lucas face followed by a three piece combo. Since Lucas was on Lore side of the hood he knew he was out numbered, so he walked off and jumped on his phone.

Five minutes flat, if that, Lucas came back with a mob of people, all concealing weapons. Since they were from the same hood they passed the guns to the girls to hold, and fists began flying. Lore, being the person he was, took one last puff of the weed and began swinging. Blaze was on the side of me and he said, "Damn that nigga punch smoke out of his ears." I started laughing so hard. After five minutes of going blow for blow, Lore and Lucas were tired so that was the end of that. When Lucas and his crew were leaving one of them said, "Next time we not coming to fight, we coming to kill y'all niggas."

Then Lore said, "Ya'll don't want to play with us with guns." The crowd was still outside talking about the fight that just happened when the stick up kids from building 61 decided to try to rob people. But tonight was not the night, because Panic wasn't having any bullshit. He had just come home from a long bid so he still was on his own bullshit. But he damn sure wasn't going to let these punk ass kids stick him up. Soon we see the stick up kids walking on the scene with a .38 revolver Special. Then we hear some shit cock back. Panic was holding a K in his hands and he told everybody to move out of his way, because he needed a clear shot to drop them.

Panic was protecting us that night. Once the stick up kids saw that

Panic held a K in his hands, they re-thought the situation about trying to stick somebody up. So they quickly withdrew by saying they didn't want any problems. Shit I would of did the same thing if I was in that position. See nobody in the hood can claim the crown because it's always a grimy person with a bigger gun in the hood that shows you shouldn't do grimy things to people you see every day. That would be the last party Baby Cheaters would have.

   A Couple of months later, there is a New Year's party in building 300 and just for a minute, it felt like Baby Cheaters was back. CP was even there. He just came home for clapping a cop. CP caught a bid for five to ten and did seven years. CP was nothing to play around with and he damn sure did not like pigs. He would spend his time on the roof tops, calling the cops and saying that there was a shooting going on. Once the cops arrived in the hood, CP would shoot at them from the rooftop, trying to pick them off one by one. Cops would run and hide and call for backup. CP would be long gone. Girls that didn't see CP in a long time, they fell for him easily like drinking water. He was so damn slick and cool, that he instantly turned them into sluts. And they were willing participants and eager to be with him. One time I saw CP with his pants down and a girl on her knees in a staircase. Since CP been on lock down, there's been new faces on the block that he didn't know. In fact, I didn't know them either. I just had seen them around. I guess the girl on her knees was one of the new niggas' girlfriends, and they weren't having it. No talking in the hood if you going to fight. Next thing I saw punches begin to fly between CP and the new niggas. CP was getting the best of the fight, when I saw razor blades coming out. I wasn't a part of the fight. I stood in the hallway in shock watching this go down. Then I saw blood pouring out on the floor. And then I saw CP. He was left with a buck fifty on his face. CP's ass was sliced up, from ear to cheek.

   After all those years in jail, he never got shanked or gave BJ's or anything like that. Now he gets out of jail, comes home, only to get cut up in his grill. He spent so much time in the joint, thirsty for a girl, he never checked with the homeys to see which girl was with which nigga. Sometimes you gotta check when you have been gone a long time, or else face the consequences of life in the hood.

Once again another party spot shut down. Soon there weren't any more party spots in the hood, so we had to go outside the hood near the Ville, and rent out Studio 181. Studio 181 was a hood joint next to a Christian Church. It was black-owned, probably by some drug dealers, number runners, or old-time pimps. They made their money by renting out their space to young guns like us. It wasn't your typical night club like in Midtown Manhattan. You were not going to find white folks up in there, or celebrities, either. This was the hood club and the cops never came into the joint. They knew what time it was. Everybody from the hood was out of their comfort zone since we was in somebody else's hood. Guns were within arm's reach of everyone. The security on the door was letting folks in who were packing heat. At Studio 181, everything was cool for the first couple of months besides the little fist fights and shots fired in the air. Then one weekend, as life in the hood happens, it all changed.

Friday night, everyone was up at Studio 181 partying, eating, smoking, drinking, and having a good time enjoying themselves. Then suddenly, the music stops and loud voices are heard arguing. The arguments turn ugly. Folks leave the club to go outside and that's when the fights begin. I realized that the fighting was between Langston Hughes Projects and Brownsville Projects. Then someone shouts out, "Y'all niggas are pussy! Suck my dick." Immediately, a dude walked up to the person that shouted out and put the barrel of the gun in his face and squeezed the trigger.

Life in the hood was happening again. Life in the hood happens often and without warning. I was one of the few people that didn't have blood splattered on them from the impact of a close range murder. By time the pigs came, there was only the body on the floor and his friends crying over the dead corpse. Within the next few months, life would continue like this in the hood with four more killings due to everybody retaliating. You can bet that was my last party I went to outside of my hood. Disrespecting niggas, foul shout-outs, always results in an ass whippings or murder in the hood. Be aware. Keep your mouth shut.

Chapter Seven: Inside Hangouts

If you were from the hood, you got to have hangouts, especially when it rained and winter came around. Those freezing cold nights and days when no one was hanging outside, the hangouts came in handy. In my hood we had so many spots to chill at. There was damn near a spot in every building. I didn't go in every spot because it was either somebody I didn't bang with or a rat in there. It was always a shame because everyone loved me and would be mad when I didn't chill with them for that reason. Now back to my story.

Being that it was many spots, everybody would always be split up so it wasn't as much fun. There were over two spots in 30 alone. My lil man Gunnz had a spot in that building. I almost lost it when Gunnz got shot. It happened when my aunt from Hawaii came up. I haven't seen her in years. I just was telling her how Gunnz was a good basketball player and that he just needed help staying out of trouble. My aunt grew up in the hood and made it out, now living in paradise. When she visited, she didn't want to stay in the hood so I met her in a hotel in Queens near JFK airport. She said she always stayed near the airport in case of an emergency, she could jump on a plane and be out of the country if possible. So we were chilling having fun eating Chinese food and catching up with each other. Then I get a call from my grandmother asking me, "Where you at?" I told her I was in Queens and she said, "Good stay there because somebody got shot near the park." After she hung up I called Tesha to ask who got shot. She said Gunnz got shot in his arm and his back. Once I heard that, my heart skipped a beat. She said she don't know if he was all right or not. When I hear of people getting shot in the back, usually it doesn't end to well. Tesha called me about two hours later and said Gunnz is okay and that he got shot once, but the bullet went in his arm and out his back. Once I found he was okay, that was a load lifted off of my shoulder. If you were looking for them lil Pistol Boy gang niggas, you can find them in Gunnz crib ninety percent of the time. I banged with them so you could even catch me in there occasionally. That was the hottest spot that the cops were watching in the hood, so I tried not to be in there too much. But every time I went in there I knew I was coming out laughing cause' them lil niggas is so funny and disrespectful to each other.

Gunnz thought he could do anything because that was his house. One day we were chilling in the crib and Gunnz took the weed out of Freeze mouth. Freeze told him if he sparked his blunt up, he was going to violate him. Gunnz said, "Nigga, you in my crib. You ain't going to do shit." So Gunnz lit the blunt and started smoking. Soon as he turned around, Freeze smacked him in his neck so hard, Gunnz drop the blunt on the floor. That nigga Gunnz was so mad he tried to make everybody get out his crib after that. Nobody listened to him though, we were too busy laughing. Another spot was on the same floor just down the hallway from Gunnz. I definitely didn't go in there cause' the person who owned that spot, had that thing on her back, H.I.V. No one else seemed to care but me, it seemed like. I mean I know you couldn't catch it by just being around her but people was eating and drinking after her like it was nothing. Word on the street was that one of the niggas I associated with was having sex with her and living there at some point in time. When niggas I bang with would want to go in her crib, I would just wait in front of the building. I would not go inside her crib. Every time I waited in front of the building the pigs would come and harass me because they had nothing better to do. But when shots were fired they ran in the opposite direction. I'm not going to go through every spot in the hood cause' it's just too many. The spot you can catch me in the most was in building 90. That was my man Lav crib. Every time I go there, my main team was there, so I already knew what it was hitting for. I knew I banged with everyone in 90, and there was never a snitch in site. Liquor, weed, females and guns were always on deck. Since there were no snitches we could always have our luxury items and not worry about police. I mean, there was times when the police came to the door; when we were making too much noise. When the police came to the door, my heart would always drop because I was thinking, like it was over, they had a warrant to search the crib. It was never nothing more than a loud noise complaint though. You see I never was into drugs or liquor, I was always into the whole gun thing. So every time somebody brought a new gun in the crib I would play with it for at least an hour. When I say play with it I don't mean point it at people or nothing like that. I mean I would take it apart and put it back together and ask people do it match with my outfit. It was just something about guns that seem to get my attention. I remember it was like four guns in the spot and Lav, Terry and I was just sitting around talking. Then it came up that the niggas we got beef with shot Gunnz the other day. So that built up some steam and Terry was like, "Let's go put in some work." I was thinking that they almost killed him, so I said, "Let's go." We were all so eager and that almost got us locked up. We didn't think cops were still going to be outside even though Gunnz got shot two days before. Terry and I walked on the side of the school and Lav walked the fire station way to get to the other projects. The whole time we were walking, I kept tightening my belt because the gun was so heavy.

By the time Terry and I were about to enter the other hood we hear a fucking radio but didn't see no one. So when Lav called me and said, "I see them niggas that shot Gunnz near the liquor store. Should I start airing?" I tell him, "No, the police is somewhere over here." Just as Terry and I turned around to go back in our hood, a female cop comes out of the shadow and asks, "What are you doing over here? Aren't these two hoods beefing?"

Then she informed us of the shooting that happened two days before. We pretended like we didn't know and told her that we were going in the house before we get shot.

Little did she know, if she would have checked us, she probably would have gotten promoted to detective or something. My blood was still pumping, so when we got back in front of the building I just threw a shot in the air and we ran back to the spot. Two of the guns we had belong to them lil Pistol Boys. So when the block cooled down, I gave them their guns back. See, they had another spot in 80, and it was Jessica's crib. It was popping, but you can rarely catch me in there because of the females I didn't like. Soon as Spazz put the gun in the spot, we go to the pizza shop. He taps me and says, "Look! That's that nigga, Tony."

I asked, "Who is Tony?" He says, "Jasmine brother that told your cousin Tesha that he was going to slap her." So as Tony went into the Chinese store, we followed him. I asked him, "What you said to my cousin Tesha?" and he said, "I don't know what you talking about." When he said that Spazz said, "Son why you fronting now?" Then Freeze came and said, "Leave that nigga alone, he soft."

We left and sat in front of 61 Thatford Avenue to see what he was going to do. I turned around and Tony was on the phone. So I told Spazz to go get the gun from the spot just in case. He asked, "Which one." I replied, "The biggest one. What you think?" He laughed and said, "All right I'm shooting this time."

Just as Spazz was coming back I seen two people walking from down the block and I see Tony laughing on the phone. So as they got closer, Spazz kept asking can he start shooting, and I said, "No. Let's see what they're going to do."

I saw one of the guys hand Tony something and then Spazz said, "I'm about to just clap him." As Tony start walking towards us, Spazz put the gun behind his back. Tony start screaming and talking loud saying, "Y'all don't have nothing to say now, right?" And then he walks off. I say to him, "You're soft you better keep walking."

He turns around so fast with the smallest gun I ever seen in his hand and start shooting.

I never seen Freeze move that fast, I swear he was near 30 and 40 before the bullet left the chamber. Before Tony let off the second shot you hear three quick rapid shots. I stood behind the tree and screamed at Spazz, "You better hit him." He stood there shooting with a bucket hat on. I guess Tony had only two bullets because he turned and ran. As he was running Spazz continued to fire. I looked and see Tony fall and get up and Spazz said, "I got him." Spazz and I ran back to the spot in 80 and chilled for a while. When we got up there we check our body to make sure we wasn't hit. Then we started laughing. Spazz said, "I told you I got I aim. I was going to hit him."

The girls that were already in the spot, walked into the front room and asked us, "What happened?" I told them that, "I don't know, we just heard gun shots." I told Spazz to stay in the house. I was going to see if Tony died. As I walked out the building, Freeze is walking up. Freeze gives me the 411. He said that Tony didn't get hit. He just fell, and everyone is saying that they saw a tall person with a bucket hat shooting. We went back up stairs and I say to Spazz, "I thought you told me you had aim? Only thing you hit was the air." He said, "When he fell, I thought I got him." Then we started laughing. I looked out the window and I see six blue-and-white officers sitting in front of the building. We become scared and think they are coming to the spot. So we start hiding the guns. We sent the girls out first to see if the cops harass or question them. They didn't, so Spazz, Freeze, and I go down right after them. We start play fighting and chasing each other so we can move by the cops fast. That's why it pays not to have snitches around cause' we would have been in jail. But that was the old me. The new me is way different and a changed man. I still love guns. I just have them the legal way now. A couple of years later the spot in 80 was over due to Jessica moving.

Chapter Eight: Undercover Brothers

In my hood we had people who we called "Undercover Brothers." At first when you hear the word "undercover", you think of police. Not in this case: "undercover" meant the down-low, man-liking-man, gays, faggots, whatever you wanted to call it. Personally I didn't have a problem with that. I just kept my distance ninety-five percent of the time. The other five percent I would try to get them to hook me up with their female friends. I notice all gay males have a lot of sexy female friends. So for that reason and that reason only, I would never call them out of their names. So you can say that I was using them, only to get with their female friends. On the other hand everyone I hang with would disrespect them every chance they got.

I remember one summer night a lot of folks were in front of building 1570, just chilling, when this gay nigga named Vegas from building 1548 walked by. He had on a pair of tight ass pants, high heels, and a wig. Everyone didn't see Vegas until he got far away. That's when Devin came out the building and said, "Who is that girl with the fat ass." Playing a game by being funny, I said, "I don't know, go get her number." So Devin started screaming, "Yo! Yo! " Calling who he thought was a girl. So when Vegas stopped Devin looked at me and said, "Let me hold your phone so I can save her number."

I gave Devin my phone as I was holding in my laugh. I told Yellowman what I did and we both stared as Devin got closer to Vegas. We just heard Devin start screaming, "What the fuck your homo ass going stop to for, like you were a female?"

Yellowman and I started dying. I swear I couldn't breathe for about five minutes. I was laughing so hard my stomach started cramping. Devin came to us and said, "Why y'all niggas play so much?" And he gave me my phone back. That wasn't the only encounter someone had with Vegas. One day Yellowman and I was chilling in front of building 1570 when we seen Vegas went into the front door of building 1548 and Laquan went through the back door of 1548. We called Laquan and asked him was he coming back outside? He said he was going to give his grandmother her stuff and come right back out. So like fifteen minutes had passed, and he didn't come back out.

So Yellowman said, "Let's go get him and see what's taking his bitch ass so long." So we went through the back way of building 1548 to see what he was doing. Just as I was walking through the back door I see a girl I wanted to talk to, so I called to her. I told Yellowman that I was going to get her digits. He kept walking to see where Laquan was at. We both had a feeling that Laquan was with gay boy Vegas. I was talking to this shorty getting her digits for about two minutes, if that long, when Yellowman peeked out the back of the building. At first I thought he was spying on me. Then he whispered, "Yo! Come here, look at this gay nigga!"

The first person that came to my mind was Vegas. So we crept up the stairs to the second floor and peeked our heads out the exit door. I see Laquan open the elevator door and Vegas was in there with him. Then I see Laquan zip up the zipper to his pants as if he just did something. Yellowman started giggling, and Laquan looked up, and we ran down the stairs and out of the building. I never saw what happened, so I asked Yellowman what did he see? He said he saw Vegas on his knees and heard Laquan moaning. "I think he was giving him head," Yellowman said to me. So after about an hour of laughing, Laquan finally comes back outside. So he says, "What the fuck yall two niggas laughing at." So I said, "Son what you was doing with Vegas?" Laquan replies and says, "Fuck out of here! Don't play with me with that gay shit!"

Then Yellowman said, "Son, I saw you getting head!" Laquan says, "Hell, no! I was peeing, and he just got on his knees." Yellowman and I both looked at him with that "Yea, whatever face!"

Then I asked him, "Why would you pee in the elevator with a gay nigga, and you live in the building?" He couldn't answer. That's when Yellowman says, "Damn! You couldn't get head from a girl, so that's what you resort to!" I just could not stop laughing. Yellowman and I told everyone what we saw. After that day I didn't see Laquan for about two weeks. I guess he thought everyone would forget, but that was not the case.

People did start to forget about it because Luke just came out the closet, out of nowhere. One day we thought he like girls, and then the next day we see him hanging with Vegas and his gay friends. One week earlier, Luke went to his prom with a nice looking female.

I always knew it was something up with Luke. He was the only one out of us, who didn't play sports. The only game that he wanted to play was tag, so that he could touch the boys. Now that I reflect back on this story, come to think of it, he always chased the boys around and would run right passed the girls. When everyone was playing basketball he would be sitting with the girls cheering.

The funniest shit I heard was when we were playing ball and someone said, "Look at Luke faggot ass clapping his hands like a cheer leader. He looked like Carlton from the TV show Fresh Prince of Bel Air!" Everyone started laughing. Luke knew we were laughing at him because he kept saying, "I don't know what they laughing at." But he said it in an angry voice.

Like I said, I don't discriminate, but it's different when you grew up with a person and they turned out to be gay. That makes you start thinking about all the times you chilled with them together and had sleepovers and then you begin to think, what was really going through their minds?

Homeless man in the hood.

Undercover police watching the hood.

This is how a project elevator looks.

The hood daycare.

The hood where you are free to pick up trash.

One of the most busy hospitals in Brooklyn closed down.

A lot of people died in front of this building.

A lot of dirty cops in Brownsville.

People rarely go to the library in the hood.

Handball court riddled with bullets many times.

Pool in the hood, but nobody knows how to swim.

Girl shirt on the roof after being raped.

Howard Houses

One day worth of garbage.

Juvenile jail across the street from the hood.

Author's daughter chilling in the crib.

Author with his daughter Haven.

Author with his daughter Haven.

Chapter Nine: Hood Boogers Females

A lot of females were hood rats in the Projects. We couldn't live with them, and we couldn't live without them. I learned at an early age that the drug dealers and killers had all the females. Females will do anything to get attention and to be noticed. They will go so far as setting another drug dealer up, or wearing low cut shorts with their butt-cheeks hanging out and tattoos on their lower back. I mean, they will do anything. They will steal from their own mother to give to a man just to get down with the team. They would even have sex with a group of men to be protected from any danger the hood would bring.

Here is an example of what I am talking about: people from other projects would always come over to Howard Houses with their guns and shoot. The females will say, "If y'all want to go over to the other projects, I will hold the gun for y'all.

Personally, I always hold my own shit. I knew if a person get killed, there was not a single female who is going to take that twenty-five-to life bid, so I knew they were going to snitch. Don't get me wrong now, there were females in the hood that knew how to hold their own ground. You had some females who lived in the hood but they weren't not into the streets. These females kept themselves looking good and decent, by dressing nice and working a 9-to-5 job. By nice, I mean tastefully dressed, and clothes covering body parts, and appearing very attractive. Other girls thought nice represented tight pants and a cut-off shirt, showing their cleavage. In my eyes, that's a recipe for a slut. I don't think I know a female from the hood that successfully finished High School, but I don't knock nobody's hustle or their grind. I am aware that school is not for everyone, but the streets are not for everyone, either. The hood raised girls who were smart enough to go to school but dumb enough to try to sell drugs in school. Then, we've got girls in the hood that were dumb enough to sell drugs, but smart enough not to get caught. The hood is just filled with crazy females. I remember Chesse was at Cindy's house in the Bushwick section of Brooklyn and she tried to get him killed. Chesse's baby mother and Cindy were best friends so he never thought anything of it. Cindy's baby father was somebody Chesse had beef with. Chesse said he was sitting at the bus stop when he turned around and saw the folks that he had beef with, and rat-ta-tat-tat, immediately these folks started shooting at him.

As Chesse was pulling out his gun, turning towards these guys, Chesse felt a bullet ricochet through his arm causing him to drop his weapon, and he started running as fast as he could to escape the bullets from raining down on him. The cops stood on the corner, and watched as Chesse's gun dropped out of his hand, then they caught him and cuffed him. When he came home, I asked Chesse how the fuck they even knew he would be there. He said he was at Cindy's house and he heard her get on the phone but he didn't think anything of it. Chesse said whoever was on the phone asked Cindy who was there, and she said, "Wanda and her baby father."

Let me remind you Cindy is fucking somebody from Glenmore and knew Chesse had beef with them. He told me Cindy's bum ass knew what she was doing, and that she had set him up. Chesse just said every time he sees that bitch, he going to Shawn Michael's super kick her. Then he asked me if he can get a free bag of weed since he just came home from jail.

Every time I saw Cindy, I would tell her to suck my dick and that she was going to die and then I would tell her, "Bitch, your day is coming sooner than you think." Now to this day when she sees me, she walks the opposite way. Sometimes she gets balls and walks past me, or even says, "What's up?" to somebody I'm with. Cindy also had a friend name Shena, who was just as grimy as her. It seem like all the girls from Howard would date the enemy.

So one day, this guy from Howard realized who Shena's boyfriend was and slapped her across her face, very hard. So she called her boyfriend. When Shena's boyfriend came, he was too scared to go on The Hill to confront the man who slapped her. I guess he already knew the gangstas from Howard wanted him to come because that night he would have been lifeless.

Bud was an innocent person who was walking around. Shena's boyfriend walked up to him and shot him in the head. I guess he shot the first person he saw. Shena could have said that Bud didn't have anything to do with it, but the bitch didn't say jack shit.

Shena knew her life was in danger. Shortly thereafter, her family moved out of Howard. One day I was in the lobby of her old building with my gun when she got off the elevator with this nigga I knew. I forgot his name, though. I went over there because Blue called me and said, "Shena's boyfriend is in the parking lot."

I didn't see him though. So I asked the nigga who Shena was with, did he see anybody from Glenmore or Seth Low Housing Project in the hood? Before he could answer, this bitch had the nerve to say, "Damn! Y'all still beefing?! Y'all need to chill out."

I automatically put on a sour face. I didn't say what I really wanted to say. So I just said, "The beef's never going to stop." He finally answers me and said, "I didn't see anybody but the police." Then he asked if I had a gun on me? I said, "If I'm outside, then my gun is on me." He told me," There is nobody out here, so go upstairs before you go to jail!"

Now back to Shena and her family moving. The day they were moving, Bricks was on the rooftop shooting up their moving van and the furniture inside it. At first I didn't know who shot the van up. I saw Bricks the next day, smiling, and he said to me, "Yo! You heard those shots last night?" I replied, "Yea, those shots were loud."

He laughed and walked off. As Bricks was walking off, he said under his breath, "I wished I would have hit that bitch." A few months later, Shena and her boyfriend were arrested for murder. Of course when they both got arrested, she tried to say that she didn't know that he was going to kill Bud. So she basically snitched on her boyfriend to get a lesser charge. Soon her charges were dropped from murder to harboring a fugitive. Instead of getting 25-to-life, the bitch got a bid of 1-to-3.

Don't get me wrong. There were also good girls in the hood. Those females went to school, then they went to work, and after work, they went straight inside their houses. Since they lived in the hood, their choices were slim, if any at all. Those females really had no choice but to talk to a thug or hoodlum, because, if they had a boyfriend, those dudes would get beat up and robbed by the thugs and hoodlums who lived in the hood.

The good girls would eventually turn into weak girls, then sluts, and every guy would run a train on them. But they would continue to go to school, then work, and back home. Those were the females in the hood.

Chapter Ten: Family

In the hood, if you don't have family, you didn't have anything. Family don't always mean actual relatives. Family could also mean close friends, girlfriends, teachers, or even co-workers. Growing up, I was blessed because both of my grandmothers literally lived seconds away from each other. One grandmother lived in 1550, the other grandmother lived in 1570. When I needed money I would ask both of them, and when they asked if I have money, I would say, "No." So every day in school I would have a lot of money.

On the days when the school principal would call home about me, I would always hide out at my grandmother house on my father's side and tell my mother that I was spending the night there. My mother would say okay and act like she didn't get a call from the school. She'd come to my grandmother house unannounced, with a belt in hand, and I knew then what time it was. Every word she would speak coming out from her mouth would be in unison with the belt as the strap landed on my butt. I got use to it so much that I would fake cry so she would feel guilty and stop beating me with the belt. You couldn't call the cops on your mother and cry child abuse, because back in those days, your mother would give you something to cry about and something to go along with child abuse.

We called my building "The Hill", because you had to go up a long ramp to get to the building. If you were on The Hill, that meant you were family, no matter which building you were from.

Every week during summer, there was a barbeque cook out on The Hill, and anyone from the hood can come to The Hill to get a bag of weed and a burger. I never smoked weed nor drank. I knew I wanted to be somebody and I also knew that if I started smoking weed and drinking, I wasn't going to make a good life for myself. I'm not knocking other people for smoking weed and drinking liquor, beer or wine. I'm only speaking for myself and my life in the hood.

Summer time was also basketball tournaments. These basketball tournaments were called "James 'Fly' Williams" or "Big Skip Tournaments." In each division, there were two Howard teams. One of the Howard teams would always win the championships and the other teams would be sore losers and blame us, saying Howard was cheating because the tournaments were held in our hood.

Then the fighting would erupt in the hood, with each team fighting another, and these young black men would be ready to kill each other. The thing you got to understand in the hood, is that we would fight each other to the death, but when someone outside our hood had beef with someone inside our hood, we banned together like brothers. Once an outsider had a fight, we would forget that we was mad at one another, then we would join together to make sure nobody from the hood got hurt.

I remember my mother use to give me a twenty-dollar food stamp. My friends and I would go to the store and buy beef patties, a bag of chips, and quarter water which was water-down juice that they sold us kids at the Puerto Rican or Arab bodega on the corner. My grandmother on my mother's side had five kids, so there were a lot of kids running around. Six of us in the same school and we had the same last name, so everyone would get tired of hearing the Pinkard's name getting called over the loudspeaker.

I remember I was in school and I brought a box of fart bombs in and gave one to my cousin, and I kept the other two. We planned to pop them the same time during third period. Third period came, and I saw students run in the other hallway, which told me that my cousin had popped his already. My teacher was being nosey by looking into the hallway trying to find out what was happening, so I popped both of mine. Then all the students had to go out in the hallway. My cousin and I was in the hallway at the same time, dying laughing. By the time the teachers figured out that my cousin and I had something to do with the fart bomb, the period was already over.

Looking at both sides of my family, I was the only grandson with no record, so everyone considered me their favorite family member. I would always go to my grandmother's house on my father side, and she would give me anything I wanted, right after she gave me a lecture about pulling my pants up from hanging below my waist. She would always say, "You know that originally came from jail, right?"

I didn't know it at the time, but my grandmother had taught me where baggy pants came from. That was the swagger in the hood. Most cool boys wore their pants baggy.

Now that I'm grown up and mature, today I dress professionally and keep my pants pulled up. I was the spoiled rich kid in the hood, not white person rich but hood rich, I was the only 13-year-old with a dirt bike and a motor scooter. Whatever I wanted, my mother made sure I had it. Even my clothes were cool. Since it was illegal to have either a bike or a scooter on New York City Housing Authority grounds for low-income families, I was the only 13-year-old kid running from the cops, or, let's say, riding from the cops. Both of my grandmothers were angry with my mother for buying me the bike. My grandmothers were afraid and always thought that I would get hurt. My mother would respond by saying, "He's not a girl, a little fall won't hurt him."

Having each other kept us sane, because living in the hood could get stressful at times. I remember when I was eight-years-old. It was around midnight, and I told my mother I was hungry. She gave me money and told me to buy my cousin and I a beef patty and a quarter water juice and then to go back in the house. We went to the store, and then walked back to our building. As soon as my cousin and I closed the door to our apartment, we heard rat-ta-tat-tat sounds. We heard about a dozen gun shots. We were scared. Just moments before we went into our apartment, we had left members of our family in front of the building. We prayed that no one would get shot. Seconds later, shaking us out of our thoughts, we heard BANG, BANG, BANG, BANG, BANG, banging at the door and everyone screaming, utter chaos and confusion. Shortly thereafter, we learned that my aunt got shot in her leg. That's when I knew the streets were no joke. It didn't bother me knowing other people was dying and getting shot, but that all changed when it hit home and somebody close to me like a family member took a bullet.

A couple weeks after the shooting incident, another beat down occurred in the hood. It was always black-on-black crime. Anyway, I was on the other side of the hood, in the next building near 30 and 40, playing kickball. So here I am playing an innocent game of kickball. When I tried to tag another player out, I accidentally hit a girl with the ball as she was walking towards the building. Her mother had seen me around and had judged me unfairly, as most folks judge little black kids in the hood. Her mother said that she didn't like me anyway and said that I was disrespectful. She then went on to say that I hit her daughter with the ball intentionally.

Next, she began shouting and screaming in my eight-year-old face. I told her to get out my face. She then put her two fingers on my forehead and pushed me hard, forcing me to take a couple of steps backwards.

Now, this is considered a threat and a challenge to fight when someone in the hood put their finger in your face and mush you like that. I tried to keep my cool, but after she did that, I felt all my anger building up. I balled up my fist and I punched her in her face. Her husband charged me and slammed me down on the bench very hard. This was tough stuff, real tough stuff, to see two grown up adults beating up on an eight-year-old kid who was playing an innocent game of kickball.

Lucky for me, a family member name Money was coming to give me some food and he saw how everything had unfolded and happened. Immediately, Money began beating the man, stomping and kicking him in his face, which caused the man to hit his head on the side of a parked car. He was dazed. The man was looking around, but the rest of his body was not moving.

While he was on the ground, everyone riffled through his pockets to rob him, and then someone ran to The Hill to get my mother and aunts. As the girl's mother was helping her husband up, my mother and aunts jumped on her and stomped her out. Then one of them threw bleach over the lady and she began screaming for her life. The cops pulled up on the scene and arrested my mother because she wouldn't stop, even after the police were present she continued. My mother's attitude was that no adult man or woman had the right to beat on her child. The police officers released my mother around the corner because they understood the length that any parent would go through and what they would do to protect their child.

So far, I have not mentioned my father or my uncle. They were there in the hood at the same time, and then they weren't there at the same time. Since my birth, my father and uncle have been in and out of prison. However, when things happen in the hood to our family, they would know about the situation within the hour. The only good thing about them being incarcerated was I would go to visit one of them and get to see both of them, since they were in the same prison. My father was supposed to have been home years ago but he has a short temper. He didn't take shit from anybody, not even the correctional officers.

I remember my friend Darius and I was chilling in the hood, and one of my cousins walked up and said, "Yo you heard about your pops? They just added more time to his sentence." I replied, "Nah, why? What happened?" He said that my father beat up seven correctional officers and broke one of their noses. Then Darius said, "Damn! Who the fuck is your pops? Bruce Lee?" I called him dumb in a jokingly manner, and we both laughed about it. Nevertheless, I love every single person in my family, no matter what they have done or did not do. That was life in the hood and, besides, that's what this chapter is all about: love and family.

Barcelona Brownsville: Life in the Hood

Chapter Eleven: Gatherings Holidays

Holidays! Holidays! Holidays! Everybody loves holidays, but holidays don't always love folks and situations that go on during the holidays. A holiday in the hood was a sight for sore eyes! Holidays were when you could get the entire family together, and tragic events such as death.

Here's my holiday story in the hood. When the family was together, OMG, we created so much laughter, filled with joy and many happy memories. We enjoyed being with each other so much that there were times when we wanted to get the whole family together. We made up a holiday or planned an event filled with food, music, jokes, smiles, and laughter. Growing up, I went to my family reunion just once. Most people at the reunion were not blood family, but we all felt like family and very close to one another.

Let me tell you about black folks and the "last minute thing." Now with black people everything is a last minute thing. You'd think that they never heard of planning ahead or in advance. One time we were having a cookout on The Hill when someone came up with a bright idea to have a family reunion at Bear Mountain the next weekend. Now in order to get the family and friends to participate, you must spread the word and get it out there by mentioning FREE FOOD, ALL YOU CAN EAT! And right then and there, one week later, a family reunion was happening in Bear Mountain State Park.

During the bus ride to Bear Mountain State Park in upstate New York, kids were excited with joy and talking non-stop about what they wanted to do first. As we were nearing our destination, I looked out the bus window and even now, I can remember the deep peaceful feeling of the mountains and serenity looking back at me. I was leaving behind the concrete jungle of the hood, the hard life of jagged edges and rough pavements, gun-shots, crooked cops, thugs, pimps, whores, crack heads, and homeless, hungry folks. Just for this day, I could escape. Just for the day, there was a feeling rising up within me that I like, and years later as I would grow up into adulthood, this life was what I wanted. I kept my dreams silent and locked in my heart. My eyes continue to take in the scenery of acres and acres of lush mountains and to remember every detail.

Bear Mountain State Park is situated in rugged mountains rising from the west bank of the Hudson River. The park features a large play field, shaded picnic groves, lake and river fishing access, a swimming pool, a zoo and nature, hiking, biking and cross-country ski trails. I could smell fresh cut grass instead of dry dead withered grass back in the hood, clean air I breathed in which helped my asthma, instead of the hot pungent smell of dead bodies littered on roof tops and human feces and pollution mixed with smog. My wide-eyes could see the swimming pools and I knew that I could swim without worrying if broken glass would be in the water to cut me. There were hot tubs, lakes, and it seemed like there were hundreds of folks that I may have seen once since the day of my birth.

Suddenly, the bus stopped, and the parents was barking orders, telling us to get all the bags and carry them to our area. By the time the parents turned around to look, we kids acted like we were in a track meet. We began running across the grass, then jumped in the pool. Everyone that was in the pool before us, they got out quickly. Were they frightened? Did they see how hungry we were for a taste of life other than our projects as we knew them? I think they had never seen folks like us from the hood before. Oh well, I thought to myself, but that didn't stop us from having fun, enjoying ourselves and performing back flips, somersaults and dives into the cool deep aqua-marine water. We must have stayed in the pool for hours, losing all sense of time, until we noticed that the sun was going down and it was time for dinner. Exiting the pool, our hands and feet were wrinkled, but everybody knows, black doesn't crack, and soon our skin would be back to normal.

It was time for dinner, and the elders began to introduce their children to family members. I wasn't in the mood for meeting and introducing myself to family members.

I just wanted to have fun. Next my aunt said to me, "This is your cousin."

I turned around to see who my aunt was introducing me to and I was flabbergasted. I stood there with my mouth wide opened. There stood in front of me this person that I had seen before. This person and I had been in school together, in the same class. I remembered that I was not nice to her, and so I just stood there for what seemed like eternity, gathering my thoughts together. When we returned to school in the fall, she would tell everyone in school that I was her cousin and she felt proud and strong, knowing that as her cousin, no one would bother her. I guess you could say, I too, never did bother her again.

Now back to the family reunion. There were hundreds of people that I have seen around the hood and they were family, but I hadn't known until then. There was so much food spread out on the picnic tables that I didn't know where to start, so I made me a huge plate and piled all the food on it, making sure that I got some of every food item that was there. That was my first mistake; I forgot that everybody can't cook. My second mistake was to let people see me throwing food away. Folks were watching. Then I heard a voice, "I'm telling! You're throwing your food away!" I replied, "Shut up! You're always snitching!"

After dinner, we all went into the hotel, where all the kids went into one room, all the parents in another room, smoking and drinking, and the religious parents in another room talking about Church. Once we were alone, we instantly began jumping on the bed, while watching wrestling. It never fails. And it seems that there always has to be at least one bone cry baby in the group. Everybody was performing wrestling moves on each other, and next thing we hear is somebody crying, saying they got stone-cold stunner. That's a wrestling move, when somebody punches you in your private part, and then pull you to the ground by grabbing your neck. And now his neck hurt.

The girls were playing, and acting, tougher then some of the boys. I turned around, and one of my cousins kicked me in my head and started screaming that he was Shawn Michaels. Shawn Michaels was a wrestler, whose favorite move was kicking people in their face. I hit my head on the wall, and the pain made me sit out the rest of the night. I was always one of the toughest kids around, but that night, my head was pounding. I had to sit with my eyes closed. It seem like any little light I saw would make me get a headache.

The next morning I was the first one awake. I went and got a bucket of water and poured it on my cousin who kicked me and began screaming, "I'm Aqua man." He jumped up screaming as if he was really drowning. By the time he realized it was me who had thrown the water, I was already sitting next to my mother like nothing happened.

Staying in the hotel, we were given free breakfast. When someone went to get their breakfast, we would pour salt in their soda. The first time our joke worked like a charm.

The person would drink their soda and spit it out on the table. This caused us to get into trouble. But that didn't stop us. The next couple of times, we would start laughing before they would drink their sodas, and by our laughter, our behavior told them that something was up, and they would not drink their sodas.

After breakfast we all went to the hot tub. We made everybody that wasn't with us get out. They got out because I'm guessing they were scared. The hot tub was right next to the pool, so you know what that meant. We would get in the hot tub first, come out and then jump directly into the pool, not knowing that when we hit the water, we would be freezing. After being told repeatedly by the security guard to stop going into the hot tub, then jumping into the pool, then getting back in the hot tub, he finally said to us that we couldn't get in the pool for the rest of the day. We were angry. We didn't want other kids to have fun swimming in the pool and we weren't allowed to swim in the pool.

So to make up for it, when other kids that we didn't know went to go in the swimming pool, we lied and said they were with us. The guard would tell those kids to get out. The security guard realized that we were lying on the other kids that went into the swimming pool, and we, who could not go into the swimming pool, fell out laughing. He then told them that they could go back into the swimming pool.

The next day, it was time to pack up and head back to the hood. We all ate breakfast and was ready to hit the road. Now, you know we weren't leaving Bear Mountain State Park without taking a souvenir. Everyone boarded the bus. As we took our seats, folks began revealing their gifts. Family members were pulling out food, toothpaste, towels, soap, out of their pockets, pocketbooks, pants, shirts, bras, whatever. Once back to Brooklyn, New York, I would not see most of the folks again until Thanksgiving.

When Thanksgiving came, everyone would begin to talk about how much they needed to go on a diet, and at the same time, they would be at the gobble table, going back for thirds. Was that their way of small talk, or lying to themselves when there was an eighteen course meal in front of them, and diets were of no use this Thanksgiving Holiday?

If I knew you that meant that I was at your house for a plate. I would go to both of my grandmother's houses and eat up a storm. I would stay at one grandmother's house and eat, then play video games. I would convince myself that I was hungry less than an hour later. So by the time I got to my other grandmother's house and was about to eat again, I would have to sit in the bathroom on the toilet for hours.

One time, I sat on the toilet for hours, and nothing would come out. I got scared and told my grandmother. She gave me a spoon of something white to swallow. It went down easy, yet tasted like vinegar. I didn't know what it was, but it had my stomach bubbling. Then she said, "If you have to fart, it is best that you fart on the toilet."

I'm thinking to myself, like, what? That makes no sense. But when that time came, I listened and I was on that toilet for hours, lighting the bathroom up. When I came out, it was eating time. I would load up my plate with ham, macaroni and cheese, candy yams, collard greens, turkey, stuffing, potato salad, rice, and ziti. And when I finished eating, I ate dessert, which was banana pudding or cheesecake. After that, it was toilet time once again. We would have leftovers for five or six days, and I would do the same thing over and over again.

My mother would say, "I know you tired of eating the same thing every day," and she would try to throw the food out. With the leftover ham and turkey, I would make sandwiches or salads or just fry them and eat it. The same thing would happen on Christmas, but there would be more food left over. Folks didn't come around for the food but because they expected gifts, even if you never saw them that whole year. I did the same too, but I was a kid, so that excused me. I would go to every family member house possible to see what they had for me. I would go from Brownsville to Bedford Stuyvesant and act like I was just in the area. Usually we set up Christmas dinner at one of our family member's crib, so we knew where to find everybody. Everyone would bring the gifts to one house, and that would cause conflicts, because there would be a lot of gifts addressed that read, "To MOM." So every mother would open the gifts, and someone would scream, "I got that for my mother, not you." We would pull out the camera and record the whole Christmas day.

People were eating and opening presents, and people were running for the bathroom.

One of my cousin's was impersonating my grandmother. He was acting as if he were in Church, saying, "Praise the lord! Praise the lord!" and didn't know the camera was recording. So the next day, when we plugged up the camera to the TV and watched the footage, he got a chop to the neck from my grandmother.

New Year's celebrations were just about the same: food and family all over again. Seeing the same people over and over again, people would play by saying, "OMG! Why do y'all keep coming over? I'm tired of seeing y'all." or "What do y'all want now? We don't have any more money for y'all."

New Year's was a little different, but a little more exciting. There were New Year's parties all over the hood, so we would run into everybody at the parties, and they would be pissy drunk. At around 11:50pm everyone would go outside and walk around the hood making noise. The minute the clock struck midnight, everyone started waving their guns in the air and began shooting to celebrate another year that they made it alive and out of jail. Niggas in the hood would start hugging, saying they loved each other. Twelve-thirty rolls around and everyone is back in Baby Cheater's or whatever party they was in.

The next morning folks woke up, saying, "How did I get here?" or "Where am I at?" That's when you know you had a good time. Without family and friends, you wouldn't have as good of a time, so I enjoyed every moment with my friends and family.

Chapter Twelve: Gangs in the Ville

When you think of gangs you usually think of the Bloods, The Crips or even the Latin Kings. In the Ville that wasn't the case whatsoever. In the Ville each hood had they own gangs. The gang in my hood was called "Pistol Boys." And that name came about because everybody in that gang had shot somebody or had gotten shot.

Personally, I didn't believe in gangs or group activity. But from my reputation in the Ville the cops just automatically thought I was a part of that gang. I had love for everybody in my hood, so if I saw anyone in need of help, I would help. And that was often, since we were the most hated hood in the Ville, all the other hoods linked up together against us. Like when Trell and Pistol boys were on Watkins in the store, and the Brah Boyz from Glenmore Plaza had them trapped. They called me, and within five minutes, I was on the corner with my gun on my waist, and we all walked back to the hood. That same night, the Pistol Boys and I mobbed to Glenmore, but on the way over, we saw the cops sitting in the car, so we turned around before they could see us.

Another project the Brah Boyz was associated with was Seth Low. In Seth Low, they had a gang called GRN which stood for "Get Right Niggaz!" They were all the same to us. We wanted them all dead, just like they wanted us dead. The only difference between them was that I personally knew everybody in GRN from going to school with them and chilling with them, a few years back. They were older then the Brah Boyz, so I didn't mind warring with them.

It seems as if all the young cats were eager to pull the trigger, to make a name for themselves. It's crazy, because before every hood decided to make they own gangs, we use to fuck with each other. Just a few years back, I remember members from GRN, Brah Boyz and Pistol Boys stole a yellow school bus together and was driving around the Ville for, like, five minutes before the cops was on us.

Dmoney from GRN was in the hood one day, and we were doing

dumb shit, walking around with guns. We were young and just wanted to shoot someone, anybody. So I gave Dmoney the .380, and, the first crackhead we saw, Dmoney shot him in the leg. That shit was mad funny to us back then. That was before anyone use to smoke or drink, so we went to a spot in the hood and just laughed about it. Even when I said, "What if he died?" Everybody laughed harder.

We didn't have a clip for the .380 so we would just put one bullet in the gun and walk around. I finally showed this older nigga from the hood named Troy the gun and he said he can get a clip for us in a couple days for thirty dollars. A couple days passed, and he showed us a bag and said, "It's in here." We all looked at each other and said, "How much you got?" We made excuses why we didn't have money. When Troy heard that he got mad and said, "Y'all lil niggas got me walking around with a clip, like, I can't go to jail for this." Then he walked in the building. We never saw the clip, so we didn't know if he was lying or not, but we never ended up getting it. We just stuck to putting one bullet in the chamber.

A couple weeks later Darius got beef with the Loyal To Us (LTU) niggas from up The Hill. I didn't think it was that serious so I didn't bother walking around with a gun. That night after I left Darius, Shawn from LTU banged on Darius door around 2am. Everybody was asleep. He stood at the door, banging for about ten minutes. Finally, Darius' stepfather wakes up and screamed, "Who the fuck is it?!" Just as he was getting close to the door, all you heard was gunfire. BANG! BANG! BANG! BANG! Four bullets flew through the peek hole. One bullet grazed Darius' stepfather on the arm. He then ran down the steps, and when he got to the first floor, he saw Shawn. At the time, he didn't know what was going on between Darius and Shawn, so he asked Shawn, did he see anybody run out the building? Once Shawn said no, Darius stepfather told Shawn that he bet not find out that was him who did that.

Next day, the block was flooded with cops, but I was risking my life, as I still was walking with my gun in my pocket. It was a little quarter water, so you couldn't notice it. Around 2:30pm, Darius and I went to get something to eat from his house. I guess that's around the time the cops switch shifts. I didn't know, so I said, "I'm leaving the gun up here when we go out." Darius said, "I'm going to play basketball. Anyway, nothing's going to happen." We got downstairs and saw no cops but we heard people playing ball in the park. When the two of us reached the park, we saw people from the hood playing, so we automatically started shooting hoops.

After about ten minutes of playing basketball, I got tired and went to get a drink from the water fountain. As I looked up from the fountain, I saw Shawn walking towards Darius, who was running for the ball with his back towards Shawn, so he didn't see Shawn. I started screaming at Darius, "Darius! Darius, watch out!" Darius thought I was talking about someone trying to steal the ball from him. Then I said, "Darius, run he's behind you!" Darius turned around and saw Shawn walking towards him with the gun in his hand. Darius threw the ball and ran. Shawn chased him and shot one time, and the gun jam. He continued to give chase as he tried to fix his gun.

Darius just had a surgery on his back, so he couldn't run as fast as he would have liked. I just look on in disbelief, because I couldn't do anything else. After Darius got near me, we both ran out of the park towards the circle. The whole time, this fat dick head cop was watching everything, and still he started to chase us, after he saw us running for our lives. As the cop was talking to Darius and I, out of nowhere, it felt like the entire 73rd precinct was surrounding us. They asked us a thousand questions, and we told them to suck our dick and to ask their partner who was shooting at us.

When they let us go about five minutes later, we heard four gun shots. I saw Darius's stepfather right after that, and he said that was him, shooting at Shawn. Come to find out, that was Shawn, shooting out of the window. The cops saw where it came from and raided his house and locked him up. I told Darius, Shawn knew what he was doing. He wanted to go to jail, because he knew he was good as dead.

Next couple weeks, everything was back to normal. We still had to worry about the Brah Boyz coming to the corner shooting, because that's the closest they would come. Shooting from that corner, they hit a lot of people though. It wasn't intended, though many times I watch them shoot with their eyes closed, or even turn their heads. Once again a lot of people were getting shot but no one was dying.

That all changed when the Pistol Boys joined forces with "The Mobb" from up the hill and the "Blazers" from down Pitkin Avenue. So now, more people were getting shot, and people were dying from their bullet wounds. Myself, personally I didn't trust anyone, especially if they weren't from the hood. So when I came to the hood and saw new faces, I would just shake my head.

I told every member of the Pistol Boys that joining other people would be the reason they fall. I started to distance myself from every team because I didn't want to get caught up with all the beef that they would bring to the table.

Before you knew, the problems were worse than before. I use to walk to the A train on Rockaway, but that got to be nearly impossible. If you was from Howard, you couldn't go anywhere without a gun.

One day, I'm sitting in the park, and I decided to walk to the store. I walk past four kids that I had never seen before, and they were moving funny, kept looking around and pacing back and forth. I was in the store, ordering my food, when I heard five gunshots. I looked out from the store and saw the same kids I had walked by, running with a gun. The kids slowed to a walk after they put the gun away, and the cops drove right past them. I watched from the store to see where they were going and I saw them walking in the building on the corner near the liquor store. This is also located near Glenmore projects.

That same day, two older people from near the liquor store jump my little man Jermaine and injured his leg. I was chilling in the crib and I heard banging on my door. It was Drayton, crying, "I think them niggas just broke Jermaine leg! Let me hold your gun!" I told him I didn't have a gun in the crib, because I thought the cops were going to rush my crib, but if they were going to go to Glenmore to put in work I was going. I quickly grabbed my black champion hoodie and walked out the door. I was thinking it was going to be, like, four of us.

Once we got off the elevator and walked out the building, I saw at lease thirty people, all dressed in black, with mean mugs on. Out of thirty of us, there was one gun and one female, so you already know who was holding the gun down. We split up by time we got into their projects. Everybody in their projects started to run as soon as they saw us, so we quickly gave chase. We chased them passed the liquor store and stopped. We stood in front of that building and I saw them run into the other day, and two of them walked out with their hand on their waists, pretending as if they had guns.

Being from the hood, we all ducked behind a car, because we were expecting them to pull out a gun. They fucked up when I saw their hand and no guns. That's when I screamed out, "They're bluffing! There's no gun!" We jumped out from behind the car, but just as we were about to whoop them out, we heard sirens. Everybody ran, except for me, I didn't do anything, so I thought there was no reason to run. The cops pulled out their guns fast and told me and the two boys that were from that building to get on the floor. Once they searched us, they picked me up from off the floor and asked me for my address.

Once I told them, they said, "You're from Howard? What you doing over here?" I told them, "I didn't know I had to have a reason to walk down the street." Then they ask the two boys what happened and one of them said, "Those fucking Howard niggas going to come over here, starting shit!" I said to them, "Oh y'all snitching," and walked off. The whole time, I didn't realize there was a crowd gathering. So when I walked off, there were about twenty people there, looking like they wanted to kill me. Even Dmoney was there. He was the only person that didn't take his eyes off me the whole time. So I waved my hand as I was walking, telling them to come on, follow me and watch what would happen. I got back to the hood and saw more people than we started with in black.

Drayton asked me, "Why the fuck you didn't run with us?" Then he asked me what the cops said. I told him they didn't say anything. Jermaine's brother Ryan said, "Let's go to Jimmy Jazz store, Nate works there." As we were walking through the hood on our way to Jimmy Jazz, we noticed the crowd was growing. They didn't ask where were we going or why. They just were down for whatever. As we walked down Pitkin, everybody that saw us just kind of stared, or kind of ran in the opposite direction. Now there were about fifty people, walking in a crowd with one girl and one gun. We walked passed two people on bikes and I felt they were grilling me.

I was feeling like nobody could touch us right then, so I said, "What the fuck y'all niggas looking at?!" Everyone turned around and walked toward the two people on bikes. When Ryan got close to them, they knew him and said, "What's good with ya mans' wilding right now?" Then Drayton says, "Y'all lucky Ryan knows y'all."

We continued walking. I didn't trust them, so I kept looking back to see what they were doing, and they kept looking back at us. I looked to see which way they were going, and they made the first left. We finally get to Jimmy Jazz. Freeze and I was the first to walk in. I didn't see anybody downstairs, so I started to walk up the steps. Then Freeze says, "Isn't that that nigga Nate right there?"

It seems that he saw me walk in and tried to hide behind a rack of clothes, because earlier that week I slapped him, when he was with his girl. I turned around and approached him. As I did, his co-workers stood on the side of him. I ask him, "Why y'all niggas fronting?" As I was talking I was clapping my hands in a angrily way. He acted like he didn't know what I was talking about, so I started slowly getting mad. I said it again, "Why y'all niggas fronting?" He started walking away. Before he can even take a second step, Freeze right hooked him. His co-workers tired to jump on Freeze. As they walked by me to try to get to Freeze, I started giving everybody left hooks. I guess they thought they had us out numbered, because all the workers started running towards us, even females.

As I started backing up to avoid any punches, I saw the whole hood running in the store. Everybody ran in our direction and started swinging. A girl worker tried to stop Ryan, he hooked her, and she dropped. In the midst of all the commotion, Freeze was snuffing Nate.

Then I see Spazz take a razor out his mouth and started cutting Nate in the back of his neck. I looked up and saw a crowd across the street looking at us and I screamed, "Yo, we out!" We all start running out the door.

Some old man was trying to lock it, we bum rushed him. When he fell we begin stepping on him to get out the door. Something told me to look back, and as I did, I saw some big nigga with dreads tussling with Freeze, and Freeze was going wild but he couldn't get loose. He was knocking over all the racks of clothes to try to get away. I wanted to go back in to get him but I already knew the cop was coming. It wouldn't have made sense for both of us to get locked up. Plus I was eighteen so I wasn't coming home.

We were outside the store, hoping Freeze get away, when Nate ran out with a pole. Everybody started screaming saying, "Now, you fronting, right?" Drayton said, "Give me the hammer. I'm going to pop this nigga." Then Nate went back in the store. When he turned around I saw the back of his shirt was soaked in blood. Drayton said, "We out before the cops come." He looked at me and said that we couldn't do anything about Freeze right then. We started walking back to the hood but we split up so we wouldn't get noticed by the cops. We saw three cop cars and an ambulance flying pass us and we watched them stop in front of Jimmy Jazz.

I say, "Yo! We need to get off this street A.S.A.P!" So we made the next left off the block. We ran up that block and we made that right and were near the 73rd precinct. I was thinking to myself, okay, we should be good. So we started walking. We were one block from our hood, when we heard a voice, saying, "Yo! Yo!" I turned around to see who was calling us, and it was the two niggas that was on bikes. I already knew what it was, so I kept walking. Drayton stopped and said, "What happened?" So I had no choice but to stop, too.

One of them replied, "Didn't y'all niggas just try to front on us?" Drayton replied, "Nah, that wasn't us." Then the other boy took his gun out and said, "That was y'all niggas a little while ago." He then said, "Matter fact, where y'all from?" Drayton answered, "From the Ville." And Spazz brother said he was from the East. I was the only one sitting there quiet and just watching the niggas on the bike hands. He then asked Drayton if we fuck with them Amboy niggas? Drayton answered, "Nah, we got beef with those niggas, too." After that, we all three walked off. I kept looking back because I was not trying to get shot in my back.

We finally reached our hood. Soon as we reached the hood we saw four cop cars flying though the hood as if they were chasing somebody. Not even a minute later, my phone rang, and it was Spazz, asking, "Did you make it to the hood safe?" Because the cops just chased him.

I told him I just got in the hood and I was looking at the cop cars now. He told me everybody was at Jermaine crib so hurry up and come up there. We all three started walking towards the building when a cop car started backing up towards us with their sirens on. We looked at each other and took off. We all ran through the grass because the cars couldn't chase us. I slammed the building door shut and ran up the stairs to Jermaine house.

Once at Jermaine's house, we all called everybody's phones to make sure we all were good. That was when my phone rang, and it was Freeze, calling from the hospital. I asked him, "Why was he there?" He said that he had to get stitches because somebody cut him on his lip. The first thing that came to my mind was, "I hope Spazz didn't make a mistake and cut him." Then he said, "Those bum-ass workers cut me, and those niggas spanked me." I asked him what the cops said. He replied, "Nothing." Somebody had to come get him, so he could come home. He then asked me to come get him, since I was over eighteen. I told him no, they might try to lock me up, because I know we all were on camera. Five minutes later, Freeze's grandmother called me and asked if I could go get him. I told her I wasn't in Brooklyn because I didn't want to tell her the real reason I couldn't go get him.

The next day we were the talk on the Ville. Everybody was saying the Howard niggas was on some other shit. At 2:30pm that day, around the time school was getting out, my little cousin Joe called me from school. I answered. He said he needs somebody to come pick him up because those GRN boys were waiting for him in front of his school. I was already with four Pistol Boys, so we just walk to his school. I was going to run and get my gun but I didn't want to waste any time and have something happen to Joe. So by time we get to Joe school, everybody was looking at us because they knew why we were there. Then Joe ran out of the school and said, "They all just walked that way. It was, like, a hundred of them."

I was thinking, he was lying. I was thinking there were only about ten of them, so I said, "Let's go them, then!" We ran across the street and up the block. I didn't see anybody, but Joe did. Then Joe screams, "Y'all niggas pussy!" And they all turned around. There really had to be at least a hundred of them because, they took up half the block. School safety had seen us running and were following us, but we didn't notice them until then. It was like everybody in GRN saw my face, and their face lit up with excitement. Everybody started pointing at me, saying, "You finally stop hiding, we've been looking for you!" So I told them, "Suck my dick!"

They all started walking toward us, so I crossed the street to get a better view of them. I turned around to see none of the Pistol Boys were with me. I looked ahead and saw half of GRN chasing them. The other half were focused on me, but school safety was behind me. As GRN walked toward me, I was slowly backing up.

One of them said, "That's not police. Let's get him!" They all just started running toward me, and school safety put their sirens on, but that didn't do anything. The first one to reach me, I swung my left hand as hard as I could and connected with his face. He instantly dropped.

I was thinking to myself, "Damn! His jaw has to be broken!" I kept backing up, and they seemed scared to come closer to me after that. I looked behind me, to see one of them trying to creep behind the car to get me, so I kept acting like I didn't see him until I was close enough to hit him. I finally did get next to the car he was hiding behind, and when he jumped out, I punched him in the nose, and he fell into the street.

Just as I punched him, an unmarked cop car put the sirens on, and the whole GRN ran off. That's my first time I ever was happy to see the cops. When they got out of the car, I said, "Thanks. Y'all saved me." But the officer grabbed me by my shirt and said, "Shut the fuck up! I saw you hit that boy in the face!" I replied, "I know you saw all of them trying to jump me, so I defended myself." The lady officer then asked me where I was from, and I told her Howard. The male cop then said, "What the fuck you doing over here, then? You must be looking for trouble." I told him, "I didn't know it was a law that said I had to stay in my projects." He let me go, and they both said, "We better not see you again."

I ran back to my hood and I saw Ryan and two other people walking. They said that they were just about to go to Joe's school. Then Ryan said, "What happened, because I just saw Blue flying, in the hood?" I told him, "I didn't see Blue, but those GRN niggas tried to jump me." As I walked through the projects, I called my man Scott and told him what happened. He said he was coming. Just give him five minutes. I told him to be careful, because GRN were about a hundred deep, walking around.

About five minutes later, I saw Scott walking through the hood. As I was walking towards him I see Spazz gets out of a cab and start speed walking. By this time the whole hood already heard what happen and a crowd started to grow.

Scott came up to me and said, "You should violate those Pistol Boys niggas for running." Then he said, "Just slap them niggas a couple times." Spazz walked up to me and said, "Where those niggas at?" I said, "It happened on Pitkin." He then walked into the building to get his gun and a girl, and they walked toward Pitkin. Soon as Spazz walked off, a grey Impala pulled up. It was those same two cops from earlier. The lady cop says, "You came to Howard to get your people. Now y'all plan on killing somebody," I told her, "We were just chilling. I'm not worried about what happened earlier."

Soon as I said that, Scott tapped me and said, "Isn't that GRN right there?" I looked, and there was a crowd walking our way. We were about fifty deep ourselves, and the cop car was behind us, so you couldn't see it. Three people started walking ahead of the crowd, coming our way. I figured those were the three with the guns. So everybody started walking toward the three people.

The guy cop ran to the car and called for backup and the lady cop ran in front of us and started yelling at the three GRN people telling them to go back the other way. I heard somebody from GRN say, "Who is this bitch talking to?" As they kept walking somebody spotted the badge. Then I heard somebody say, "Oh shit, that bitch police." Next thing I see is GRN dashing back inside their own projects.

No more than two minutes had past when at least six cop cars pulled up. These weren't regular cops. They all had on suits with shoes. They had the nerve to say that we had to break up the crowd and go in the house. I hate cops, so you know I had to say something. I said, "Nigga, we pay rent here, so we don't have to go anywhere." He said, "You must want to be arrested for disorderly conduct"

Once we heard that we all walked towards the building and all the cops followed behind us. I told the girl with the gun to walk in the building first. Once she got in the building, the rest of the crowd started walking toward the building. Soon as we gained a little distance from the cops, we all turned around and screamed, "Suck our dicks!" and ran in the building. I didn't come back outside until it got dark. I almost fucked around and got arrested messing with them gangs in the hood.

Chapter Thirteen: Gun Play

After the age of seven I really couldn't tell the difference between right and wrong. I saw people doing so much wrong, I actually started to believe what they were doing were right. Once I saw my first body at the age of seven there was nothing else that would ever compare to that. So when I saw other crimes, they would not affect me at all.

I remember what happened with Yellowman, Nose, and I like it was yesterday. We were playing basketball in the green court in front of 80 Osborn. We were playing Utah. For y'all who don't know what Utah is, let me explain it.

Utah is a basketball game that you could play with as few as two players or as many as fifteen players. The games went up to one hundred points, but we counted by fives, and the first player to reach one hundred won. Or, if there were a lot of people playing, whoever got the lowest points got eliminated when somebody else reached fifty.

Well, back to the story. We were playing Utah, and I was losing. I was a sore loser, so when Yellowman or Nose got the ball, I would foul them for no reason. Soon they both figured out what I was doing and they started passing the ball to each other, making me mad. So I quit, and they got bored with just the two of them playing.

When the game was over, we walked to the arcade room on Osborn and Pitkin. Nobody can beat me in Marvel versus Capcom, so now the shoe was on the other foot, and they were mad. After spending the next two hours in the arcade room, we began walking back to shoot a little bit of hoops, when suddenly we heard a loud screaming noise. The first thought that came to my mind was that somebody was getting raped or something.

Just as I looked up to see where the scream was coming from, a body hit the ground. Leaving a loud impact and turning heads as far away as two blocks from the scene. As Yellowman and Nose approached the body, I looked up at the top of the building and saw two figures look over the ledge and then run back. I looked at the body from a distance and I saw all types of fluid, guts, and brains all over the pavement.

Seconds goes by and the crowd, starts growing large. There was not a cop or ambulance in sight. When you're in the hood you can expect no help to arrive for at least twenty minutes. I'm guessing he would have never survived the fall anyway.

Police came on the scene and didn't investigate. They just said it was a suicide, so they wouldn't have to do paper work, or look for a suspect, whom they knew they wouldn't catch, anyway. Once the Sergeant arrived on the scene, then the police officers started to do work. I heard the officers say it couldn't have been a robbery because he had money and his jewelry was still on. After that the ambulance put a white sheet over the body and police put yellow caution tape around the scene. They then put a big white sheet from the gate to the building blocking our view. We couldn't see what they were doing. You know, one of those sheets as if they was shooting a movie or a photo shoot?

Next thing we knew, we heard a whole bunch of clicking. Some lady screams, "OMG! They're snapping his bones back together!" And she ran off in disgust. Everyone was saying, "WTF is she talking about?! They are snapping pictures of the body." That day changed my life forever.

Since then, I have seen thousands of violent crimes, and none of them would affect me, not one bit. But it was at that moment that I looked up and saw two people on the roof looking down that I knew the violence was real and I wanted out as soon as possible. Before the age of ten I had witnessed over eight dead bodies lay on the ground. It only got worse as I grew older. Being that I was staying out later and I was able to do more things.

The closest I ever came to death was at the age of fifteen. There were always new people moving in and out of the hood. Dread, a new person in the hood, decided he wanted to sell drugs and he didn't care who had anything to say about it. He had a daughter and he was doing anything necessary to take care of her. For a couple months nobody said anything to him but he had no intention on stopping.

One day, the block money was slow, and Shotty didn't like how his pockets felt. So he went upstairs and came back down with a .357 automatic handgun. Yellowman, being a dummy, went following behind Shotty, not knowing that would be a mistake.

So Shotty ran up on Dread with a grip on his gun and said, "Give it all up!" Dread gave it up peacefully, and Shotty told Yellowman to come take what he wanted. Once again, Yellowman being stupid, say he wanted his phone, and Dread handed over his phone. Once Dread handed over his phone, Shotty began pistol-whipping him. The next thing you knew, Yellowman started punching Dread. Out of nowhere, a crowd joins in and begins beating up Dread.

That next day we were playing Corners in the elevator in 1548. Corners was a game when a bunch of people got on the elevator, and whoever didn't have a corner, got beat up. There were at least twenty of us that day, so that meant sixteen people were getting beat up.

I ran down the stairs and waited in the back of the building, because I didn't feel like getting punched. As I exited the building, Dread was standing there with three people, and two of them were on bikes. Dread quickly started reaching toward his waist, when a family friend named Deuce said, "He doesn't have anything to do with that," meaning I had nothing to do with the beat-down that happened the previous day.

When Yellowman and everybody finally came out the building, Dread took his gun off his waist and told all of us to sit on the bench. He asked us, "Where the fuck is Shotty at?" We said that we didn't know who he was talking about, but he kept insisting that we did know. Dread's face was swollen, so he couldn't really see, and that was a good thing, because he didn't recognize Yellowman. If he had, we all would have been shot. He then went over to his two friends on bikes and said, "Let's make an example and shoot these lil niggas!"

That's when Deuce said, "I will go knock on Shotty's door, 'cause I'm not going to let you kill these kids." Shotty didn't answer the door, and Dread said, "Let that nigga know I'm looking for him," and walked off. Five minutes later, Shotty came out the back of the building and said, "Where's he at?" As he was talking, he cocked back his .357. I told Shotty that Dread had left the hood already.

Shotty came up to me and said, "I was asleep. God didn't want me to kill anybody today." Then he started showing off his gun and said, "Y'all know I would have shot him in the middle of his head, right where his hair first started growing at." We all started laughing and, as soon as Shotty went back in the crib, we all went in the house.

The next day, after Dread's face was healed, I was with Yellowman near the circle. When Dread walked up, looked hard in our faces, and said, "Y'all were with Shotty that night, right?" He went on to say, "Y'all lucky, y'all little niggas!" As he began walking off, he turned around and said, "Matter of fact, call that nigga before I shoot both of y'all!"

We both reached for our phones so fast and dialed his number. Yellowman got through to him and told him what was happening. Shotty told Yellowman to tell Dread not to go anywhere, that he would be down in five minutes.

So Dread went to hide in the back of the building, so he could shoot Shotty when he came out of the building, not knowing Shotty could see everything from his windows.

Shotty came out the front of the building, dressed in all black, and called my phone and asked me, "Was Dread in the back?"

I quickly said to him that Dread was by the blue car near the library. The next thing we saw was Shotty running toward the library, shooting. Then we saw Dread running. Shotty got down on one knee and really started shooting. During this shooting spree at Dread, Shotty screamed, "Don't run now!"

When Shotty clip was finished, he got up, walked to Yellowman and I and said,

"I thought he had a gun?" We said in unison, "He did!" "So why the fuck didn't that nigga shoot back, Shotty said. That was the last day we saw Dread in the hood, I tell you that much.

Just because Dread was gone, the drama didn't stop. We still had to worry about them Brah Boyz from Glenmore. By then I had moved to PA, but I still was connected, so when something happened I always got the call. Blue called me and said the Brah Boyz just came through the hood shooting. So I asked him did he want me to send some help over there, and he said yeah. So I called my little cousin Rich and told him to get some guns and some shooters and go to Howard the next day.

That next day, Blue called me when he was with Rich, and he said they were about to go shoot up Glenmore. As soon as I hung up from Blue, my phone rang, and it was Rich, screaming in excitement, saying, "It's about to go down! There are about a hundred of us, and I got my goons on deck, plus with your goons, we are about to turn it up" I said, "It sounds like a party!" And Rich said, "Yeah, we are about to throw a going-away party!" I laughed and told him to be safe and I hoped nobody get shot or locked up and I hung the phone up.

About thirty minutes later, Blue called my phone, out of breath, saying, "Yo! Jermaine from Howard just got shot in the foot." I couldn't really hear him clearly, because he was talking fast, yet I understood. I asked him, "How, and where was he, and who was he with?"

Blue said, "We all mobbed to Glenmore with one gun, and one of Rich's men had it, and he didn't know who to shoot at. One of the Brah Boyz started shooting at us, and hit Jermaine in the foot."After that, my phone started ringing like crazy. I answered when Drayton called. He said, "I think Rich's goon shot Jermaine in the foot by mistake, because he didn't even know who to shoot."

I said, "All y'all were together. He knew not to shoot anyone from Howard." My phone beeped, and it was Rich on the other line. I told Drayton I would call him back. I switched over to answer the line that Rich was on. He says, "Son, I'm not helping those Howard niggas out any more. They got me tight, saying my goon shot Jermaine." He then went on to say that "Drayton was mad because I didn't want to give him my gun to shoot because I didn't trust him.

People told me that Drayton would have tried to take it after the shooting was over.

So now Drayton was saying that my goon shot Jermaine, but we all saw the Brah Boys shooting at us." He finally stops talking and lets me speak.

I told him, 'Well, don't fuck with them anymore, because I sent you over there to help them, and they are saying shit like that." I asked him was he good, and he said he was great, but those Howard niggas were out of luck if they needed help again.

I called Drayton back and said, "Rich is not helping anymore, because he risked his life and freedom to make sure the people from the hood were good. He came to help, and now y'all Howard niggas were saying his goon shot Jermaine." Drayton said, "It looked like he had done it."

Just before I hung up, I told Drayton that I was not sending any more help over. I said to myself, "That's what I get for trying to be nice and protect the hood, when I'm not even there." But once again, shit like that happened when you were living life in the hood.

Chapter Fourteen: Gone But Not 4gotten R.I.P.

Shit is mad crazy when you are with someone and less than five minutes later they are dead. That's something you don't want to get familiar what feeling. After a while I got familiar with it. After a while when I heard that someone got killed I didn't even cry. That lack of feeling very much affected me. As a matter of fact, it made me the strong person I am today, and at the same time, in the process, it made me an animal.

Before the first time my eyes saw a person get killed, my thoughts on death were naïve. I thought you could only die from old age or a disease, or something like that. I thought that way because I knew a lot of people who were getting shot, but they did not die. So, once I saw someone get killed, that experience changed my entire view of life.

I thought as long as I lived in the projects, there was no way out. So when people tested me that would usually lead to a fight, and then a shootout minutes later. I didn't understand what was happening to me until my friend got killed in two-thousand and eight. I still remember the last couple of days that I spent with Cereal before he was killed. The shit was so funny, every time we were together.

The night of August 2nd, Cereal, I, and, like, five other people, were macking in the hood. Sitting on a bench, when out of nowhere, Brain asked Blue, what size was his beef? Everybody just paused, and then started die laughing, and in the midst of laughing, I was trying to say that he was gay, but I was laughing too hard to say it. After the laughter stopped, Brain said he was asking what size were his beef and broccoli boots?

Cereal was the pimp type. I swear every girl that walked by us, he would talk to her. Since we were laughing, we couldn't see that a girl had walked past us. By the time we realized, the girl was already at the back of the building. The door was locked, and Cereal ran fast to open it for her, but she said she was waiting for her man, and he said, "I'll slap your fatty!" If we didn't know her man, we probably would have beaten him up. He came out, saying, "Y'all young, horny niggas need to chill."

The next thing we knew was that we heard a bunch of females arguing. We turned around and we saw Pretty Gangsta Ladies (PGL) mobbing. Cereal's girl, whose name was Shorty, was a part of that click, so we followed them.

Not long after we followed them, it was on and popping. I saw hands swinging everywhere. Then I saw my cousin fighting too. She was a part of P.G.L, Half of the girls they were fighting with ran off, which left the other half to get stomped out. One of the girls tried to break it up, and Cereal's girl, Shorty, said, "Don't touch me!"

The girl then tried to leave by climbing the gate, which was a dumb move. Just as one of her legs was over the gate, she got a haymaker to the face, which knocked her off the gate into the dirt. Cereal and I could not stop laughing. The nigga Blue got mad 'cause we were laughing. He didn't even know the girl. He helped her up and walked her to the corner. When he came back he said, "I got her number." During all of the commotion I lost my work. Brain found it and I gave him a free bag.

The next day we were all outside, and the girls P.G.L was fighting the night before came back. Since it was early in the afternoon, there was a lot more people outside than it was last night. So that was a wrong move for the girls. The scene look like a mob chasing ten people. The crowd stop chasing the girls on Pitkin Avenue.

As we were standing there, I saw some people I had problems with in the past. These were the members of GRN and the Brah Boyz. So I said to them, "Why the fuck y'all niggas near this hood?" They acted like they didn't want any problems. Then I said, "I'm about to violate these niggas!" The crowd said, "Once you began swinging, we are going to do them dirty!"

I don't know why I let them rock, but we should have stomped them out. One of them was about 4'10. Spazz said, "You should have slapped him, because we would have thrown his little ass in the air somewhere!" Once we got back to the hood, I went to get my gun because I knew they were going to come back. So I was riding around on my bike with my gun on my waist. Then I saw Johnson, and he said, "Let's go to the other side."

By that, he meant we should go to the other projects. So I rode through my hood and dropped the bike off in the park. When we entered Glenmore, I took out my gun and cocked it back and then put it back on my waist. Johnson said, "Isn't that Murphy, the nigga who came through the hood, shooting, the other day?"

I said, "I don't know what he looks like." But then I looked and saw somebody I had beef with, and he had a baby in his hands. We were behind them, so they didn't see us. I didn't care about the baby in his hands. The only thing on my mind was walking up to him and shooting him in the back of the head.

Just as I pulled my gun out, something told me to turn around. I turned to see a cop car drive by. Luckily, they didn't see the gun in my hand. So I walked out of the parking lot to see where the cops went, and as I stepped out of the parking lot, I saw three more people I had beef with, walking in. The cops were about twenty feet away at a red light, so I let them three people walk by, not knowing one of them had a gun.

Once the light turned green, I pulled my gun back out. As I stood, watching the cops drive off, someone started shooting in my direction. I could see the bullets hit the wall in front of me. With my gun in my hand, I just sprinted across the street, back to my hood, and I heard the cops' sirens as they backed up.

I ran through the park and dropped my gun in the garbage, as I saw an army of cops running my way. I ran through the back of my building and walked out the front of the building to see what was going on. I looked toward the park and saw a bunch of cop cars. Then Johnson said, "I think they found the hammer if you threw it in the garbage."

Dante came to me and said, "Rashawn's aunt told the cops the gun was in the garbage." He then asked me if that bitch was a C.O or some shit like that? All I could do was shake my head. I thought everybody in the hood liked me, plus I was protecting the hood. This time, it wasn't even me shooting.

Then as I walked off, I saw Cereal, and he said, "Nigga, how you tried to shoot somebody that close with a sniper?" I called him dumb, and we laughed. I told him I was about to go to Jason's house. Cereal walked in the other hood direction with Lewis.

I didn't think anything of it. I thought they were walking to the park or the store. I walked to my boy Jason's house, and he gave me a different shirt to put on. I started calling people in the hood to see what was going on. I wanted to see if the cops were looking for me. So I called Terry to see what the word in the hood was.

The first thing that came out of his mouth was, "Yo! Who killed Cereal?" I said, "Nigga, what the fuck are you talking about? I just saw him, five minutes ago." He told me to go outside and see. I went on Jason's balcony and saw Roy, and I asked if Cereal had gotten killed, and he said, "I don't know. I just know he got shot in the back or something."

So Jason and I ran outside, and we saw everyone crying. I asked everyone, "Where is Cereal?" They told me he was gone. Then Ty a girl from the hood asked me if Cereal was okay, and I told her that I didn't know. Yet, everyone kept saying he was gone. She started crying and ran into the building. Now everyone was walking around the hood, either mad or sad and looking for revenge as soon as possible.

I lost the only gun I had earlier that day, so I didn't know what I was going to do. I began to think. I knew Leonard had a car, and Prince had a gun, so the three of us got in the car and headed to the area where Cereal was shot and killed. It didn't look like a crime was committed. There was no yellow tape or a police officer in sight. We didn't see anyone we were looking for and it was getting under our skin. Just as we were heading back to the hood, we saw the girlfriend of this guy we wanted dead. So we pulled to the side of her and showed her the gun and said to her, "Tell your boyfriend his time is soon."

Then we pulled off in a hurry just to make a scene. Still until this day, if I see the person that killed Cereal, I'm going to kill him. Of course, people in the hood know who did it, but we didn't want him in jail. We wanted him dead!

Between two-thousand and eight and two-thousand and nine, I lost more than ten people that I was close with. In two-thousand and eight between March and June I lost three people alone, including my mom's boyfriend. Every time I see or hear the word Poconos, I think about my mom's boyfriend Rasheen. We were supposed to go there the day he got killed.

When I first met Rasheen I didn't accept him because I didn't want anyone to be with my mother. I was overly protective, especially after I found out he just came home from a fifteen year bid for a body. But after a while I grew to love him. I started looking at him as a father figure just because he was always there for my mother. I remember when I had a parent teacher conference; Rah and mom went to my school.

The next day at school, all the teachers were asking me what my mother and father did for a living, because they had matching minks on. I told all the teachers the same thing: don't worry about it, just know they were both getting money.

That summer Rah and Money had a few altercations. The last altercation led to Rah shooting Money in the hand. I knew after that it was going to be an all out war between them. Every time Money would come give me and my brother money he would have a car full of people, and they always looked like they were hunting to kill someone. So my mother's birthday came around and it was close to Valentine's Day, Rah took my mother, my brother, cousins, and I to the Pocono Mountains for the weekend.

That was my first time seeing fake snow, but it felt so real. We went from riding the snowmobiles to the snow tubes. That was the first time I felt like we were a real family. We would go to the hot tub and jump straight into the freezing pool. Until this day I haven't had as much fun. There was an all-you-can-eat buffet for breakfast, lunch, and dinner. We even had a real fireplace in our room. We didn't know what we were doing. When we lit the fire place the whole room was full of smoke. So Rah wet a towel and threw it over the fireplace to put the fire out. It was a good thing that it was our last night there, or else there would have been a shootout between Rah and the hotel police, because I know damn well he wasn't going to pay the extra fee for starting a fire. Everything felt unreal until the weekend was over and we were back in the hood.

Once we were back in the hood, we went back to ducking the gunshots. The next day after we got back, Rah got locked up for drugs. Since he was on life parole, things didn't look good for him. My mother bailed him out the next week.

On the morning of March 19th 2004, I woke up and told Rah, "Let's go to the Poconos!" And he said, "Let me go make some more money. Then we're going up to the Poconos!" He left out of the house that morning, and that would be the last time I would see him alive. I was going to a party in the hood, when I saw my mother speed walking pass me. I asked her where she was going and she continued walking and said to me, "I'll be right back."

I didn't think much of it until the next morning when I was at my grandmother's house and I heard my grandmother say, "Life is short." Then I asked my grandmother where Rah was at, and she said he got shot. Still no one ever told me that he died. So when I went outside, I saw my mother hugging Donovan and crying at the same time. I walked over to where they were and I asked Donovan why my mother was crying?

He just kept saying, over and over, "You know what happened. You know what happened." I said to him, "No, I don't know what happened!" He then said to me, "Stop lying!" Then I asked him where Rah was at, and he said he got shot.

I asked him what hospital was Rah in? And he then told me that Rah had died. I told him to stop lying, and he said, "What you think your mother is crying for?" I couldn't do anything but walk back to the bench and sit in shock.

That whole day people kept coming to me and asking if it was true about Rah. I would just shake my head yes. I was holding back tears. Since I was used to Rah sleeping at my house I was scared to sleep at home for a while, so I would sleep over at my grandmother's house. When I finally went back home, I would think I saw his shadow walk by my room. That whole month I would have dreams about him being alive.

The cops told my mother that it wasn't a robbery because his money and jewelry were still there, but his phone was missing. That next week strange things started happening. We would get private phone calls to the house and when we answered, they would hang up. My mother would go to Rah baby's mother house and they would get private phone calls asking for my mother. My mother thought it had to be the person who had Rah's phone but she remembered our house number wasn't in his phone so she was scared. She thought people were following us around to see if we were talking to the police. So I started carrying a gun with me everywhere I went. I even took my gun with me to school. Every time we were in the car I would look through the windows to see if we were being trailed.

Finally it was time to lay Rah to rest. My aunt Sandra couldn't hold herself together. She was crying so hard she leaned on the casket and nearly tipped it over. When she did that, his body moved, allowing me to see the hole on the side of his head. Seeing the hole in his head just made burst in tears. I didn't want to see him like that, and I couldn't believe somebody would want to take his life away.

The word on the streets was that he owed over twenty-thousand dollars to his connect. That was hard to believe because prior to him being killed he spent ten thousand dollars on his and her mink coats for my mother and him. The next couple of days after the funeral I would be in the library, and Chesse would ask me who killed Rah? I said that I didn't know, and he would go on to say, "Nigga, you know Money killed him."

I didn't know what to believe anymore. I was too depressed that Rah was really gone. I felt bad for my mother because that was the first time in years that I really saw her happy. A week after that on March 30th Dee got killed in the hood. I remember the night before Dee got killed, I was chilling with him behind 1548 under the bridge where the scaffold stood. It was Dee, Lore, a bunch of older niggas and I, being the only young person there. They was laughing, smoking, and drinking.

Every time somebody walked past that they didn't know, they would grab their guns, just in case it was about to go down. Around 9pm, my mother called me to come home, because it was a school night. I got home around 10pm that night and went straight to bed. The next morning I heard my mother on the phone while I was lying in bed. Her screams woke me. I heard her speaking frantically into the telephone, "Is he dead?" and "Who was he with?"

So when she came into my room that morning, I pretended like my asthma was bothering me so she can take me to the hood and I can be nosy. And it worked. I didn't go to school that day. When we pulled up in the hood we saw a crowd around 1580. As we were walking towards the crowd, my mother told me to take my sick ass to my grandmother's house. Soon as I got in the house I ran to the window to be nosy.

My grandmother asked, "Did somebody get shot?" and I told her yes. She said, "I heard four shots but I thought that was housing maintenance doing work on the buildings." Everyone was surrounding the building because Dee's body was still on top of the scaffold. As I was looking out the window I heard the crowd screamed, "OHHH!"

That was the coroner finally pulling his body down off the scaffold. It took three hours to remove his body. I still think that if they would have gotten him down sooner he would be alive today. But in the hood the police and ambulance take as long as they want, especially if it's a black person who gets shot, it seems like they take even longer. Exactly three months after Rah got killed, Lore got killed.

About a year before that, Lore was with Rigga up the hill somewhere, smoking in the car, when someone opened fire on the car and hit Lore in the back, about an inch from his spine. Every time when he walked around with his shirt off, I saw his wound, and it would give me chills.

Lore was one of the few older niggas in the hood I looked up to, not only 'cause he would give me dollars almost every day, but 'cause he would hold the whole hood down. I remember when P.G.L. was fighting some girls from Seth Low, and we were fighting the boys from Seth Low. Lore started slapping everybody, including the females from over there.

Then he would say, "Now go get your older brother or pops and tell them I did it." Later on that night, everyone was chilling on The Hill. When we looked near the library, we saw a group of people coming. I thought they were about to start shooting, so I ran into the building. As they approached The Hill, I just started seeing fists fly, and I came out of the building to watch.

After it was all over Tramaine from Seth Low was still on the ground. He got up after about five minutes and ran. The next day around noon I was in playing basketball, and I saw Lore and three older niggas from Howard walking fast. About five minutes later, I saw Tramaine with three people from Seth Low walking inside the hood. Shortly after that I heard somebody scream, "They're right there!"

Shots were fired after that. It felt like the shots were right next to me ringing loudly in my ears. I estimated there were at least two-hundred shots fired. The shooting lasted about three minutes but seemed to go on forever. When it was all over you could hear the parents screaming and calling out looking for their kids. The buildings were filled with bullet holes and so were the cars in the parking lot. After all that rampage of shooting there was still not a cop in sight.

Finally, we saw cop cars in the parking lot, followed by an ambulance truck. Everyone started walking to the parking lot to see whose body lay on the cold concrete ground. As I got closer, I realized the body lying stone cold dead was Tramaine from Seth Low housing project, riddled with bullet holes. The ambulance people finally put him on a stretcher and placed him in the ambulance.

Not even an hour had past when the word spread in the hood that Tramaine had died on the way to the hospital. Some people in the hood couldn't believe what happened, and other people were saying, "That's what he get for fucking with those Howard niggas." That whole year, there were gunshots almost every day. The parents would make sure their kids were in the house before dark.

Then came June 19th 2004, everyone was in the park. I was playing ball with Darius. Then Lore, and Derrick came into the park with a bottle of Henny and sat down. Lore said, "Y'all little niggas ain't shit in ball. I'll bust y'all asses!"

I told him that he was fronting and that he was drunk. He said that he didn't get drunk and that Henny was like juice to him. Then my mother pulled up to the park and said to me that we were going home. I asked her if Darius could come with us, and she said, "Why you asking like he doesn't always spend the night?"

When we got home, Darius and I were playing a game, and I heard my mother on the phone, and she said, "Stop lying! Who was he with? Oh, my God! They shot him in the head?!" My mother quickly left the house and said to me that Lore got shot and she will be back. Darius and I were hoping that Lore didn't die, but then Yellowman called me and said, "It's a wrap. Those niggas killed Lore. He was with that bitch nigga Derrick."

Derrick got shot only once in the back. The word in the hood was that Derrick was closer to them niggas then Lore was. The next day everybody was on The Hill, and Lore's man Tyreek was ready to go to Seth Low and kill everybody. He was even ready to kill Derrick because it looked like a set up. Lore would never have gone over there for nothing, and then to get caught over there without a gun. Tyreek was on a motor scooter the whole day with a bag on the handle that held his gun.

My uncle had to talk sense into everybody and said, "It's too early to react. They're going to expect that and so will the cops." The next couple of days, the hood was crazy. No one could walk through if nobody didn't know them. An unknown couple was walking about their business through the hood when Tyreek walked up to them and pulled his gun out. He made them give up all their valuables and told them to get the fuck out of his hood.

Finally it was the morning of the funeral and everybody on The Hill was dressed in black. Some people were drinking water. Some folks were already crying, and some were even drinking liquor. We all left together. Some of the folks took cabs and limos, and some walked to the funeral home. Everybody got there before the service started, so we all were reminiscing in the lobby of the funeral home.

When we walked into the service, people were already there. I was guessing those were his family members. Then some old man just started banging his hand on his leg as he was walking towards the casket. When I saw that, I just sat all the way in the back and then I heard Tyreek say, "Oh, Hell, no!" Then he walked back into the lobby. When Tyreek finally came back in, he just looked at Lore in the casket, because he still couldn't believe he was dead.

Everybody was okay until the sad music began playing and folks started crying. After the service was over some people went to the burial site and others went back to the hood. I couldn't see someone being buried as if he were a flower, so I walked back to the hood. Once everybody got back to the hood, we changed our clothes and posted up on The Hill, drinking and remembering the fun times we had with Lore. That killing was the last gun-related death we had until December, 2006.

About a week before Christmas two-thousand and six, I was at home in PA, looking at porn, when the phone rang, and my aunt's number comes up. Usually, she doesn't want anything, so I didn't answer. She kept calling, so I paused what I was watching to answer her call.

She didn't say hello or anything when I answered the phone. She said excitedly, "Wake your mother up!" I heard my mother say her favorite words when there's a killing, "You lying! Who was he with?" Once she got off the phone, she told me Rigga got killed in the East part of Brooklyn. She said some nigga tried to rob him for his bracelet and he didn't give it up.

Rigga was a nigga I looked up to. He was always getting money and always dressed in the newest shit. I remember one day he was driving a Navi and then the next day he was in a Benz. It was like money came so easy to him even though he worked so hard for it. Rigga was the only person I knew in the hood that hustled every drug but he never directly touched anything. So when the feds rushed the hood they couldn't lock him up for anything.

Those of us from Howard felt like we were the most hated hood in Brooklyn. The niggas we had beef with would go to Rigga to see if he can squash it. They knew he had enough power to make sure no one got shot.

The first time my niggas and I decided to go to Glenmore and let them have it, Rigga was chilling in the park as we walked by. I felt that he knew what we were up to because we never go to that hood. As Casey, Chesse, Lav and I walked by him he just looked at us. I went to the corner and saw a crowd of people and we were about to shoot until Lav said, "Two police walkers are in the crowd."

We walked back to the hood, and Rigga asked us what we little niggas were up to? I said nothing, and he said, "I know y'all are up to no good." We laughed and walked off. As we were walking through our hood we said, "Fuck it! We're going to go back tomorrow, since the cops are out there."

Since Chesse didn't lived in Brooklyn, he said that he was leaving and not to go back without him. Like ten minutes if that long, after he left we had our minds set on going back. Once again we walked pass Rigga, and he just observed us, not saying anything. Rigga stood up to see where we were going.

I was looking out this time, so I stayed in the middle of street to make sure no cops were coming. Casey was holding the gun and Lav looked to see if the cops were still there. I'm guessing the cops weren't there 'cause Casey passed the gun to Lav and he started squeezing.

As we all walked back through the hood, Rigga's girl pulled me to the side and asked me if my mother knew what I was out there doing? Then Rigga told her, "Leave him alone. He's good." The next day, my uncle asked me, was I with them when they were shooting? Before I could answer, Rigga said, "Nah, he was in the park the whole time."

Later in the week, Rigga gave me some shells for our gun. The next day we were on The Hill and Rigga asked me did I see some bullets behind the tree? Earlier that day, Blue told me he found bullets. So I told Rigga. I guess Rigga asked Blue about the bullets, and Blue said that he didn't have them. Later that night, I saw Rigga and he said to me, "You going to get that little nigga hurt if he doesn't give me my shit."

Early the next morning the park was crowded. Folks was relaxing or playing ball. Blue was on the first bench and I was on the last bench. Rigga walked in the park pass Blue and was about to walked out until he saw me. Rigga grabbed me and tried to take me to Blue. I resisted him at first and didn't want to go because I didn't want to seem like a snitch, but at the end of the day, I felt that Blue wasn't going to do anything with the bullets.

When we finally were in front of Blue, Rigga said to me, "Didn't you tell me he got my shells?" I said, "Yeah." Rigga said, "You and your pops are going to get hurt if I don't have my shit by tonight." I'm guessing he got his bullets, because nothing happened to Blue or his pops. That same week I was on The Hill and I heard two gun shots coming from near the park.

Next I saw Matt running toward buildings 30 and 40. Matt was a neighborhood gangster. Not far behind him, I saw Rigga giving chase with a gun in his hand. That was the first time I ever seen Matt running from anyone.

The next couple of weeks would be normal. Everyone in the hood was cool, even Rigga and Matt. Then one night, all that changed over a dice game. Rigga had a grand in the bank and he rolled a duce. Tyreek was up to roll next and it took him about eight rolls to finally get something. Tyreek bet the whole stack.

So when the first dice stopped on one, the second dice stopped on two, and everybody looked on anxiously, as the last dice kept spinning. It finally stopped on three, and that was it. Tyreek had aced out. He had to cough up $1,000 cash he didn't have, so he quickly pulled out a black handgun. He then told Rigga that those dice were tricked and that there was no way he would keep acing out. Rigga just looked surprised that Tyreek would even pull a gun out on him and then not even use it. Rigga also knew that Tyreek didn't have the money to pay him.

The next day I was outside. I could always tell that something was up, because The Hill was empty, and The Hill was never empty. I sat on the bench by myself. People started coming outside, but no one stayed out long, because they knew something was about to go down.

Finally, Tyreek and his man Nelson came out and sat on the bench.

Tyreek had a bag in his hand, and he kept looking around nervously. Five minutes passed, and Nelson's phone rang. He placed it on speaker, and Rigga was on the other end.

Rigga said, "Tell your man Tyreek he's as good as dead, and it's not smart for him to be outside." Tyreek then screams, "Suck my dick!" Then he grabbed his bag, pulling it closer to his body. I got up to look around to see if I could see Rigga anywhere. I then stood close to the building, just in case bullets started to fly. Nelson hung up the phone and said, "Rigga's furious. He doesn't want to hear anything."

I walked to the park to see who was in the park. I saw Rigga and his brother walking toward The Hill, looking mean. I didn't hear any shots go off so I thought nothing happen and the beef was squashed. The beef was indeed squashed but Tyreek paid the price for pulling out a gun.

That same night, there was a party and I see Tyreek in the party with a bag of ice on his face. He finally removes the bag and he had bruises and cuts to his swollen face. Come to find out Rigga and his brother took turns pistol whipping him.

A couple of days later Rigga got locked up for something and he had to do a couple months in the joint. When he came home I saw him one last time before death knocked on his door. I was walking near the park, and Rigga was near the library, when he said to me, "Yo! Duts!" Duts was another nickname folks called me in the hood. He went on, "Where's Money at?"

I told him that I didn't see Money that day. And that was the last time I heard Rigga's voice. I couldn't make it to the funeral, but it was said he lay there with a smile on his face. The hood would never be the same after that. Rigga was loved by everyone. He never had enemies just haters. A year passed by and no one was killed. It felt good to see everyone breathing from the year before.

Two-thousand and eight came and beef was out of control. There were shootings all the time, even in broad daylight. I had to take my little cousins to school some times and I had no choice but to walk with a gun on my waist, because there were shootings as early as eight o'clock in the morning. With all these shootings, I thought someone else was bound to get killed but that wasn't the case. People were getting beat down, shot, and even cut up, but no one else died. The same thing happened in two-thousand and nine. This was a daily occurrence.

Nobody was getting murdered until June 12th, when Bang got killed. You would have thought it would have been somebody we were beefing with to kill Bang, but that wasn't the case at all. It was some new nigga name Anthony who moved in the hood who murdered Bang. He was a cool dude, but I didn't trust him. One night Anthony asked me for 9mm shells and I told him I didn't have any, even though I did. He was so cool everybody in the hood let him eat. He sold pills so he wasn't really cutting anybody's throat and he often gave those Pistol Boys erase niggaz pills for free. It seemed like they would do anything for a pill. I guess Bang was the only nigga from the hood to feel a type of way because pills were his way to eat. In the days leading up to June 12th, the word in the hood was Bang was going to rob Anthony. It was said that when Bang said he was going to rob him, one of the Pistol Boys was there and went back to tell Anthony, and he gave them free pills for the info.

When June 12th came around, the day was nice and warm in the hood. The sun was shining. People were out and about. Then, around 2:30pm, I was home and still sleeping, when I was awakened by my mother's screaming on the phone. I had the feeling somebody had gotten shot, because of what had been going on that whole year. That's when I heard my mother say her famous words again, but this time she said them differently. She said, "You're lying! Who was he with? Did they stop working on him? Oh, my God! You are lying!" Erase period in front of I. I jumped out the bed and opened my door to try to figure out who got shot. The way she was talking, I thought it was Corey, Bang's brother because she said my uncle was with him. I came down the stairs and my mother was pacing back and forth in disbelief and shock. As I was about to ask her what happened, he said, "You know that nigga Bang just got killed." I asked her, "How? By whom?" She said, "Some nigga named Anthony from 48 shot him twice in the back on The Hill just now."

Let me remind you that it was 2:30 in the afternoon, so I was thinking to myself that it was broad daylight. He had to be on drugs or just stupid. Everybody said Anthony was rolling on E pills, because when he gave everybody a pound, he was grinding his teeth together with ashy white lips and spit on the corner of his mouth. I went back upstairs and just said to myself, "Not Bang! He can't be gone!"

My phone rang, and there was a text message from Darius, saying Bang had just gotten killed. I didn't even bother texting him back. Right after that, my phone rang again, and this time there was a call from Terry. I answered and I asked him if he was there when Bang got killed?

Terry said he heard two shots from his window and went downstairs. By the time Terry got to The Hill the ambulance was putting Bang on the stretcher. Bang's arm kept hanging off the stretcher and that's when he knew Bang was dead. As this was going on the cops were chasing Anthony driving on the highway. Anthony got caught minutes later with the gun in his car. Terry said. "No sucker shit, but I'm happy he got caught, because nobody would have ever seen him again if he got away."

In that same week Anthony's baby mother moved out of the hood because she knew her and her child were never going to be safe. The next day I read the article on the internet. People were leaving crazy comments saying shit that would have never been said to Bang's face. I think he was the most known nigga in the Ville at that time.

People were saying shit that they heard, but I knew him, so I knew they were mostly telling lies. Bang was like a little brother to my mother so I grew up watching him. I remember one time, I must have been no more than fourteen-years-old, when I was on The Hill and saw a gang of dirt bikes, just riding through the hood, out of nowhere. Bang came out the building and asked me what I was looking at. I told him that some dirt bikes just rode through the hood. He asked me was one of them yellow and I told him yeah. Then he said, "Oh that was them Langston Hughes Projects niggas." He said he would be right back, as he walked in the building.

Within two minutes Bang came down the steps with a gun in his hand and said, "Let's see them ride back through here again!" Bang walked to the bottom of The Hill to see if he heard or seen any bikes. I seen three blue-and-whites coming. I screamed to Bang, "Yo! Bart is coming!"

Bart was what we called one of the cops, because he looked like Bart Simpson. As he was walking back toward the building, he and the other cops were speed walking. Once Bang got in the building, he looked back once and dashed up the steps.

The cops looked in both staircases and the elevator and then asked me "why did Bang run, because we know who he is." I told them that I didn't know, I thought he got on the elevator. As the cops went back to search the building, Bang called my phone and asked me, where were the cops? Then he said, "Never mind. I hear their chirps in the hallway."

Bang was also a rapper. He wasn't one of those corny rappers either, he had talent, raw talent. He made sure I was in his first video that he made. I was playing ball in the park when they started filming on The Hill.

Bang stopped the video and came to the park to get me and finish shooting it. Our projects looked like Howard Day, because it was hundreds of people who were in the video shoot that day. Everyone wanted camera time so they would push each other out of the way to get to the front of the shoot. On this day, the hood was united 'cause of Bang's video.

Nowadays everybody is against their own people who they grew up with. Bang still was fucking with everybody and I think that was his down fall. When the beef was getting too heavy he made a call for us and next thing you know, we had many guns. When the beef started to calm down the guns were coming up missing. The same people Bang brought the guns to the hood for, were the same people who were stealing them. After the beef calmed down we still would have at least one gun outside in case of an emergency.

One day I was chilling with Bang, and he walked to the store and said that the hammer was in the grass if people we had beef with came. I had my own gun outside already. As I was waiting for Bang to come back from the store, I saw people ducking behind cars next to the library. So I ran to the grass to get Bang's gun because it was bigger than mines. But it wasn't there. I heard a dozen shots go off. I ducked and saw the shooters walking toward me. I grabbed my gun and just squeezed until there were no more bullets left. Bang came back and said those shots didn't sound like the fifth. I told him there wasn't a gun in the grass. He kept saying he know where he left it at.

The next day I went in the library, and since I was known by the security guard, he came to me and said, "I'm tired of these motherfuckers shooting. This time these no-aim niggas broke the window." I looked up and saw that the window was broken and just shook my head and thought to myself, "My aim can't be that bad!"

I walked up to The Hill after that and I saw Laquan, and he said that he thought that Bang stole his 38 special. He told me that he left his .38 in the building, and the only person he saw come out was Bang. I told Laquan that he should press Bang to see what he would say. I don't know what happened after that.

The next day the Brah Boyz came to our hood and were chasing people. I didn't have a gun at that time so I ran to Bang's house. He wasn't there so his brother gave me the gun anyway. I gave it to Rahmel who is one of the Pistol Boys, so he could put in some work. Soon as we walked out the building, there was a cop car approaching. We walked right past the car but then they circled and came back around. Three cops got out and told us that they wanted to talk to us. We instantly took off running.

As Rahmel and I raced towards the building there was a little girl in the way and I didn't want to run her over, so I ended up falling to the ground. I looked up and could still see Rahmel running. I figured I could get arrested 'cause I had nothing on me. In that way, Rahmel could get away with the gun. I went to Central Bookings that night.

The next day I came home, I saw Bang and he asked me here his gun was at. And I told him that I didn't know, because I got locked up. He said, "How you don't know, when you had it?" He shook his head and walked off, and that would be the last time I ever saw him. Living in the hood, every day could be your last.

Chapter Fifteen: Capital City The Burg

"The Burg," for those who don't know is the slang name for Harrisburg, the capitol of Pennsylvania. Yeah, everybody including myself, thought it was Philly. That's how boring Harrisburg is. I'm only bringing this city up because it's a part of my life. After my mother's fiancé was killed, and she saw me getting caught up in the street life, she decided it was time for a change, so somehow we ended up in The Burg. I mean it was a small city, but it still had its fair share of crime.

When we first moved to Harrisburg my mother, Darius, and I came to see where we would be moving. We had to check it out. When we saw the area, the first thing I said was, "This shit looks like the TV show, The Wire." There was a bunch of little town houses all together and people's wash clothes hanging outside on a clothing line. In New York those clothes would have been stolen the second they were left alone.

The first couple of nights we lived there, it was quiet. I went to the park and played ball and I busted them down. It seemed like everyone on the court had an ankle monitor on. There was a little boy who could not have been no more than twelve years old who was wearing a monitor. He lifted up his shirt and showed me that he had a quarter water on his waist.

The next morning I woke up and turned to the news, and in the background I could see those same courts in the park where I had been playing basketball. Someone was fighting the previous night and got shot in the head with a shotgun at close range, and the police were scraping pieces of brain matter off of the air conditioner.

"So much for getting away from the hood!" I thought to myself. It seemed like we moved from hood to hood. I thought we would move back to Brooklyn, because my mother missed New York so much, we would go back there every weekend. Once school started that all changed. Of course when you are new people are going to try you.

The first day of school students were in the lunchroom, waiting to hear their names get called to see what classes they would be assigned to. Some nigga walked up to me and said, "I'm going to need that seat, so I guess you're going to have to stand up." I told him, "You must be smoking some good shit to even think I'm getting up, fuck boy!" He said under his breath, "New nigga, think he's tough." And then he walks off.

The first thing I noticed when I entered the school and the lunchroom was that there were no metal detectors. My guess was that this school was not as bad as the schools in Brooklyn. Let me tell you though it was crazy female drama throughout the whole school year, but let me get to my name finally being called in the lunchroom.

The first couple of weeks didn't wear my new clothes and I was still shitting on everybody with old clothes. So just picture what I did when I did bring out my new clothes, SHUT IT DOWN!

Eventually all the students names had been called, and they went off to their assigned classrooms. When I got in my classroom, I sat in the back of the room to scope out the scene. Good thing I wasn't the only new person. The other three new people were from New York, so we just clicked.

We never even knew each other's name at first. We just called each other by the name of the Borough we were from. So we had Harlem, Bronx, Queens and I was Brooklyn. We didn't really chill with anyone the first week of school until Carl started cracking jokes, and I was the king of jokes so that was right up my alley. Carl was the funniest person in school, and people would try to avoid him so he wouldn't talk about them. Not me, I waited for him to say something funny to me.

Once he did, the jokes just started flowing. I had the whole class laughing so hard the teacher asked me to leave the classroom and not come back until the next day. But the next day was the same, and she couldn't keep telling me to leave, so she had to deal with it.

That's how I started talking to everybody, because the students would go around saying, "Yo! That nigga right there is mad funny!" They would point at me. People would test me, and I would get them with the jokes. This was the first school where I ever ate lunch. The food there was actually good. The lunchroom was the place where almost everything went down, from jokes to fights.

My first year at school was good. I really didn't have any problems. I passed every class except art. I was present every day but somehow I still received a zero on my report card, even though attendance is twenty percent of my grade.

The next year everything was different. All my New York niggas stayed in New York. I was solo for a little bit. Then I met Dirtball and Whiteboy. Both names are self-explanatory. I calmed down and I stopped telling jokes and tried to focus on nothing but my schoolwork. That's when Whiteboy introduced me to Latrell. Latrell was the only person in school selling everything that was illegal, and committing crimes in school. Since I was in that city basically alone I really knew nothing about how the streets were in PA. I went to Latrell to buy some weapons. He named about ten guns that he had for sale. I wanted two of them. I wanted a .22 and a 40 caliber. I was expecting to spend around $700. Once he said to give him $250 for both of them, I told him I would come get them after school.

Soon as school let out, I went to get the money and we met at a mutual friend's house. Latrell was already there, with at least five different guns, by the time I got there. I felt like a little kid in a candy store. I grabbed the two I wanted and Latrell shot them in the air to show me that they were working. I gave him the money and I took the guns. I was nervous driving with weapons in my mother's car, but it was a chance I had to take.

A couple weeks later I got a call from Whiteboy, who told me that Latrell had just gotten shot. I called Ron's phone, and Ron said that Latrell got hit in the leg, and that lil' nigga Roy did it. A couple hours later, Ron, Latrell's brothers, and I were at Latrell's home with fully loaded clips. We climbed in two cars and drove around looking for Roy. We didn't find him, and I was kind of glad we didn't, because we would have gone to jail with so many guns on us, on top of a murder charge.

The next time I saw Latrell in school, he wore a bullet proof vest and packed a gun in his book bag. I felt like I was back in Brooklyn. Now back to Dirtball. He wasn't into the streets. He wanted to be a rapper. He was all right. He did some battles and a couple of shows. I recorded his first music video.

I didn't have all the materials I needed, but I made the video with what we had. The only thing I hated about Dirtball, was that he tried everything that the rappers did. He was not an original. One time he came to school and his face looked fake. Come to find out he tried codeine syrup before he came to school. His face looked so funny I could not stop laughing. He got so mad every time he saw me he left school early. See I played too much still.

Whiteboy let me hold his DVD and I made a rule that if I have it for more than 24 hours, it was mines. So that was how all three of us started thinking. If I let somebody hold something, I made sure I got it back in less than 24 hours. That rule was a problem when Whiteboy let Dirtball hold one of his mother's DVD's, and forgot to get it back within 24 hours.

I always instigated by saying, "Damn! You let him keep your mother's DVD?!" My instigation always started an argument between the two, and they would go at it for a week. Then one day, Dirtball gave Whiteboy's mother the DVD back and didn't tell Whiteboy. Dirtball told me what he had done, so we were at my house, and I kept saying, "He deaded you on your mother's DVD."

Whiteboy just snapped and wanted to fight Dirtball. I never thought it was going to go any further than arguing since I knew Dirtball didn't have the DVD anymore. Soon as we left my house Whiteboy snuffed Dirtball in the face and they began fighting. My mother came outside and asked me why did I let them fight?

Meanwhile, I didn't know my mother was in the house the entire time listening to us. A couple of hours after the fight, we were back in my house, laughing about the situation. The same night we went out driving looking for some girls. For some reason I was the only one into white girls. We would drive into the white neighborhood and get lost and then we would have to ask for directions. The white racist people would give us wrong directions all the time. Whiteboy had the nerve to tell me that white people were the devil. I thought to myself, shit like he wasn't white. To me white girls were just less drama, but I was proven to be wrong. I'm going to tell y'all about that story later. For now, we're going to talk about all the girls we had and ran through before that story is told.

Since Dirtball worked at the movie theater, he should be getting all the girls, Wrong! I was the one setting us up with the girls. One day Whiteboy and I started texting Dirtball from a number he didn't know. We pretended that we were the girls he had met at the movies. Dirtball is so dumb, he knew he didn't meet a girl at his job, but yet he fell for it. So every time Whiteboy texted him from the unknown number, Dirtball texted me saying he got some girls for us. So Whiteboy continued acting like the girls texting and said, "Make sure you got two friends with you."

Now, what were the chances of some girl texting him, telling him to bring two friends with him? Dirtball was so dumb, he still didn't catch on. We gave him an address to meet the girls at after he got off work. I picked up Dirtball from work, and we started driving to the phony address. Dirtball was in the back seat. He didn't even realize that every time he texted the girls, Whiteboy's phone rang. When we finally got to the destination, we got out of the car and said, "We don't see any girls."

So Whiteboy let Dirtball look at his text messages, and Dirtball said, "How you get that conversation? Why does that say my name?" I just started die laughing. Whiteboy said, "I'm that sexy girl you've been waiting for! I turned and said, "You have just been punked!"

So after the laughs, I called up Rebecca, a white girl I met from Middletown, Pennsylvania. I told her to have some friends over, 'cause my boys and I are coming. We weren't there five minutes, and I saw my boys having sex with her friends. I remind you that this meeting was their first time ever seeing each other.

After the little party we had, we drove back to my house, and Dirtball and Whiteboy started pulling out stuff that they had stolen from Rebecca's house. You can't take anybody from the hood anywhere without their stealing. It was a good thing that I was only using Rebecca for money and pleasure anyway, so I didn't care. For the next six months we played our game like that with at least fifteen other white girls.

Then I met a white girl name Emma who was a virgin with no friends, so I felt that we shouldn't play her like that. No more than two weeks after I met her. She wasn't a virgin any more. I started getting feelings for this white girl even though I knew my mother didn't like the fact I had a white girl.

Emma and I did everything together, even going out to plant flowers in my backyard. Then one day she called me saying she was pregnant, but she never wanted me to go with her to the doctor which I thought was funny. Two months later, she told me that she had a miscarriage. Then a month after that she told me that she had a secret about her father. She said, "I want you to know, but you must promise me that you will not tell anyone or leave me because of my secret."

She told me that her father was going to court because her eighteen year old cousin said he had raped her. It didn't hit me until a couple months after she told me. I started thinking that her father raped her and she covered it up by saying that it was my child. Everything changed once I thought about that. Every time we argued I would say to her, "Your father raped you."

She would cry. Why would she cry if it wasn't true? Our relationship started to fall apart, so I would go out with Dirtball and Whiteboy to chill with girls. I would rarely see Emma. After that I got my gun license and I started working as an armed guard, leaving little time to see Emma. I was tired of our relationship anyway, so I just finally showed her a picture with me and another white girl. She said she didn't care.

A week later, the cops were banging on my door saying I have been harassing Emma. When they pulled the phone records they see Emma calling me over a hundred times within a week yet they say that I'm the one harassing her. What it boils down to was that it was her harassing me. A week after that I was ordered to turn in my weapons because she said that I put a gun to her head saying I would use it. So I had to pay for a lawyer to get my weapons back. Once in court

Emma started crying and I started laughing and so did everyone in the court room. After it was all said and done, Whiteboy came in the courtroom laughing and said, "I told you white girls are the devil."

To this day, I thank Emma for her stupidity. She made me realize I had the talent to write books, and during that time, I bought a new car. After that I wouldn't get close to another girl. I would go back to my old ways. Every time I would look at a white girl, Whiteboy would say, "Don't be stupid. Don't play with that demon!"

As for Dirtball, every since he found his girl, he's been acting gay. Meaning he would only come around when she was gone. He couldn't do anything without asking her first. He even had to ask her if we could chill at his crib. Whiteboy and I still talked about that day he came to school with that fake face. Now that I think about The Burg, it actually has a lot more action going on than I thought.

Chapter Sixteen: The Start of the End

The summer of two-thousand and eleven, my mother and I were on our way to New York City on a Thursday morning for my grandmother's retirement party, to be held the next evening. It was my first time back in New York since New Year's Day, and I was anxious to get to the hood because I knew I would see some action. The traffic was crazy trying to get through the Holland tunnel. It felt like we were stuck in the tunnel for hours but it was only forty-five minutes. As soon as we got out to the other side of the tunnel into Manhattan, I called everyone.

That was when Tesha told me Edward stole my little cousin's bike. I told Tesha when we see Edward, that he had better have the full amount of money for the bike. We got to Brooklyn around noon. We made a stop at my aunt's house first which was about five minutes away from the hood. When we got in, my aunt told me Edward stole the bike and he got the nerve to say somebody stole it from him. My aunt told me that she saw Edward the other day on a different bike and he said that it was his brother's bike.

Come to find out, Edward has been stealing bikes from little kids and backyards and selling them. I was thinking I had to get to the hood fast to see if I could find him. So when my mother went to use the bathroom I would sneak and take her car keys and drive off. I wasn't going to say anything to anyone. I just was going to act like I didn't know anything. Since the weather was nice and it was a hot day, I knew that everyone would be outside in the park.

I would drive up to the park and get out the car, because I knew everyone would be excited seeing me step out of the car. When I stepped from the car, folks walked up to me and either said, "Drive me somewhere!" Others said, "I see you are doing your thing!" I would never drive anyone anywhere, but I would say, "Of course, I'm doing my thing." And we would start laughing.

My grandmother would be the last person I always saw, because

I would stay outside for hours before going in the house. So she would always think I stayed in PA, because of that it made her more excited when she finally did see me. I wore new clothes and had jewelry blinging on my wrist and neck when she saw me. She said I look handsome.

But if somebody tries to take my watch, give it to them, because I can buy another watch, I can't buy another life. I screwed up my face and said, "Grandma aint nobody going to take nothing from me, they know who I am." Then I would say, "I'm going out," and she would tell me to be careful. In order for her not to worry I'd say, "I'm only going upstairs to Darius house, anyway."

Sometimes I really wished I were going to his house. That would have saved me from a lot of trouble. Soon as I left my grandmother's house, I went directly outside. There was no one outside, so I went to my man Ace's crib. He lived in the Brownsville projects, which were where some members of the GRN gang were from.

So I would circle his block before I park, to make sure I didn't see any of them standing in front of his building. After I parked the car and got out, it was kind of like I was a female swinging her weave back and forth, the way I kept turning my head back and forth, to make sure nobody was behind me. This was the way we lived our life in the hood. When traveling, we watched our backs and we watched our fronts. Just like crossing the street, you always looked both ways, and then sometimes you ran fast as lightning. And then you pray, "Feet, don't fail me now!"

I called Ace and told him to have the door open because I didn't want to stand in the hallway no longer then I had to. I mean, I wasn't scared or anything like that. I was just acting smart. Ace would be so hyped to see me, because he was my main man, but I didn't see him as much since he moved. After I walked in his crib, he would say, "I thought you weren't going to come up here because you are always saying you're coming but never come." I would lie and say, "I'm too tired to come."

Ace would then say that I should have just called him, so he could have come to the hood. He'd say, "You know those niggas on this side want your head. You know they want to kill you." I would say, "Those niggas always run when they see me anyway, because more than half the time, when they see me, they know I'm shooting."

Ace then asked me what the dress code was for my grandmother's dinner. I told him that I didn't know and that I was wearing a polo shirt with some ACG boots. He pulled out some slacks and a button up shirt and some shoes. I told him only thing that was missing was a tie and he would be ready for a job interview. We laughed about it and started playing the video game. We turned the music all the way up and turned the TV all the way down.

Less than thirty minutes later, we heard a bang at his door. The first thing that came to my mind was, that I knew those GRN niggas didn't know I was in that building. It can't be them knocking on Ace's door. Ace turned the music down and walked to the door. To his surprise, it was the cops, and they said that they heard his music while they were walking past the building. Then the cops asked Ace what was his name? Ace replied, "For what?"

One officer says, "You're disturbing the peace with that noise and that's a ticket". Then Ace shouted at the police officer, "How the fuck you trying to give me a ticket?! I never knew you can get a ticket in your own house! Man, fuck you!"

The other officer then said, "You keep being disrespectful, we will have to arrest you." Then Ace gave the cop his name, and they gave him a ticket for $168. The whole time, I was standing behind his door, peeking through the crack. Ace automatically said he wasn't paying the fucking ticket. Later that night I went back to Howard to my grandmother's house and went to sleep.

It was around 4am when I finally went to bed. It felt like I was asleep for only ten minutes when I heard loud church music and my grandmother singing. I rolled over and looked at the clock on the TV, and it was 8am.

My grandmother was so excited about having the family together for her retirement party. She asked me, "Did I wake you?" Of course I told her that she didnt wake me, even though she did, and I was dead tired. So the minute she left out the house, I turned off her music and went back to sleep.

The next time I woke up, I turned over to look at the time and I was expecting the time to be about 11am or maybe even noon, but the clock said 4:09pm. I said, "Oh, shit!" I jumped out of bed. Then I heard my grandmother's voice say, "You didn't know I was here. You must not use that foul language!"

I stood there shocked and in my boyish voice I lied, "Grandma, that was the TV you heard!" My grandmother's dinner started at 6pm, so I jumped up and started to iron my clothes. I missed calls and text messages from the whole family. Then my cousin Tesha walked in the house with a bag of clothes and said she had to get in the shower. My grandmother said, "Why the two of y'all wait until the last minute to get ready?!"

Then she shook her head and said, "Well, my dinner starts at 6." She left the house, heading to the restaurant. Tesha and I both said, "Grandma is always overdoing it, rushing us for no reason!"

My phone rang, and it was my mother, asking me if Tesha and I were ready to go. I said no and told her that Tesha was still in the shower, and I still had to get in. My mother then said, "Y'all about to get left. Why are y'all two always the last ones to get ready?" And with that, she hung up on me.

I was thinking to myself, my grandmother just basically said the same thing. I was driving us, so why were they worried anyway? Damn, women! It was 5:30pm, and now I was ready to leave, when Tesha says, "Hold on! I'm waiting for Wanda to come." Now I was thinking to myself again, saying, "She can't be serious! If we come late, somebody is getting slapped!"

I almost forgot about Ace. I was hoping he was ready. While we were waiting on Wanda, I called Ace and asked him if he was he ready to go. He said that he was not dressed, and then he asked me if I still wanted him to go? You should have seen my facial expression when he said that. I told him that he didn't have to come if he didn't want to. I said that because I knew it would make him feel bad.

Ace said he was about to brush his teeth and get dressed, and then he would be ready by the time we got there. There was still no Wanda in sight, so I told Tesha I was going to go wait in the car. While I was waiting in the car, one of the Pistol Boys gave me their new CD. I told him I was about to leave the hood for a few and that I would bring it back when I returned.

Now it was 5:46pm, and I was aggravated. No, I was damn near pissed. I called Ace, and he said he was ready. I was about to leave, when Tesha called my phone and said, "Where are you at? Wanda and I are waiting for you?" In my angry low voice I deliberately said, "I'm in front of the building sitting in the car waiting for you." She said in her matter-of-fact voice, "We were waiting on you, but we're coming down now."

That got me so pissed off that I decided to get them back. When I was driving to go get Ace, I was speeding hitting pot holes. I hit a pot hole so big that Wanda hit her head on top of the car. She said, "Oh, my God! You are driving crazy! Let me put my seatbelt on!" When we got to Brownville projects, Ace was already waiting on the corner for me. When he got in the car, Tesha and Wanda said to him, "You look nice, but you look like you are going to church."

So we pulled up into the diner on Linden Boulevard and the parking lot was crowded. After ten minutes I finally found a parking space. As the four of us entered the diner a white waitress came up and asked us if she could get us a table? Nobody answered her, and then the waitress said, "Y'all must be with the party."

I knew she was thinking some racist shit in her head, but she knew not to say it. As we approached the section where the party was being held, I saw my whole family. They had to connect four tables, so everybody could sit next to each other. I saw everybody except my grandmother. Then I looked at the table closest to my family and saw my grandmother. She was sitting with her co-workers and people from her church, so that was the last place I wanted to sit. I did not want to be preached to that night.

After my grandmother introduced Ace, Tesha, Wanda, and myself to everybody, we walked toward the rest of the family and sat down. That was when one of my grandmother's co-workers called me and said, "Here's a seat right here." Of course I didn't want to sit there, but I couldn't say no, so I just sat there with the stuck face. Then I heard my mother tell Tesha to look at how sad I looked and everybody started laughing. My grandmother finally told me to go sit with everybody else. I acted like I didn't want to, but I was glad to.

Now the waitresses were taking orders for drinks, and next for the food. The adults ordered liquor, and juice for the kids, and I ordered a mixed juice with fruit. When a waiter handed everyone their cups, all the cups were small except mine, so everyone at the table was staring at my cup. The kids even said, "Dang! He's about to get drunk!"

Wanda said, "Damn! How much what that? That looks good! What kind of liquor you have in there?" I told her it was just a fruit juice and that I paid $6 dollars for it. Everyone's liquor was $10 or more, so they were mad. They all ordered the same drink: Henny mixed with Moscato. Wanda's drink looked different from everyone else's, so she took sip of Tesha's drink. Then she called the waiter and said that her drink didn't have Henny in it.

The waiter said that he had watched the bartender put Henny in every drink. Wanda started getting loud, saying, "I know what Henny tastes like, and there isn't any in my damn drink!" The manager came out and Wanda told the manager to look how dark everybody else's cups were, because they all had Henny in theirs. I guess the manager didn't want to hear Wanda's mouth anymore, so he just went to get her another drink and said, "I made it, personally."

After that the waitress finally came to take our orders for food. I looked at the table where my grandmother was sitting at and they were almost finished eating. My grandmother had the same drink I did. Every time she took a sip, she would laugh. So my aunt said, "Look at Mommy over there, acting drunk!" Then she screamed, "Ma, Ma!" My grandmother answered, and my aunt said, "You know, they put liquor in your juice, right?"

Everybody started laughing, and some said in a joking manner, "Sister Pinkard, I know you didn't order liquor!" Their table was just about finished eating, so everyone at that table started getting ready to leave. That's when our food was just being served. By time we got our food no one wanted to eat but the kids. Everyone else asked for a platter so we could take our food home. So the kids finished eating, and everyone was going to my aunt's house for the after party. My grandmother said to drop her off. She had enough partying for one night. Ace said the same thing, so I dropped him off at home.

Once we got to my aunt's house, we sent the little kids upstairs, and the party began. There was so much liquor there I didn't know what to drink first. I'm not a drinker but I figured, I celebrate for my grandmother's retiring. After a while I started mixing drinks. I started getting so hot. That was when Tesha asked me to drive her down the block to her friend's house to get the speakers for the music. Of course we had music but you know black people want to wake up the whole neighborhood. I told Tesha and Wanda to come on, let's go.

As soon as I stepped out the door the fresh air hit me and I felt like I wasn't even drinking. The air woke me up. On our way to the car we saw Tesha's cousin Ty who asked if she could come with us? I was probably driving drunk, but I couldn't tell, and Tesha and Wanda were in the car with full cups of liquor. All I was thinking was that if we got stopped by the police, we were going to jail.

Now we were one block away from picking up the speakers, and we were also on the side of the police station, when we saw Edward on a bike. Ty started screaming saying, "Turn around! That's the bike! Turn around! That's the bike!" I made an illegal U turn on the sidewalk. As I was turning the car around, I saw an unmarked police car in the rearview. Ty, Wanda, and Tesha all started screaming, saying, "A cop right there, and we have all this liquor in the car!"

I looked at the cop as I drove by and he just kept going, so that was a relief. I drove off and caught up to Edward and said, "Pass that bike!" You could tell he was rolling. He was sweating and talking with a slur. He replied, "You see the cops right there! What the fuck are you doing?!" I said, "Son, stop fronting!" I tried to hurry up and park and jump out the car. By the time I got out the car he already rode off on the bike. I continued driving down East New York ave and he stopped on the bike and said, "You think I'm playing?"

I stopped again, and this time, Tesha and Wanda started looking through their pocketbooks and said, "Oh, he's getting cut tonight!"

As I got out again, Edward started riding the bike. He screamed out, "All right! Keep following me and watch what happens!" He rode through Howard. I wasn't going to keep chasing him because I knew I would eventually see him again. As I was circling around the projects to get the speakers. We were in the car laughing, saying he must have drunk some tough juice or some shit, by the way he was talking. So Wanda and Tesha said, "He was about to get cut. He just didn't know."

I turned on Mother Gaston and Pitkin and I saw the bike he was riding, on the ground near the corner. Soon as the light turned green, he came out of the house with two people, a black and a Puerto Rican boy. I pulled over and said, "What were you saying, pussy? I didn't hear you clearly, because you were running away."

The Rican boy asked Edward, "Is that him?" He meant me, and little pussy Edward said, "Yeah, that's that bitch nigga!" Just as I was opening the car door to get out, the Rican boy pulled out a chrome gun. I didn't see it at first. I just heard Ty saying, "Don't get out. He has a gun." I looked in the mirror and saw Ty and Wanda getting low in the back seat and then I saw the gun as he was walking towards the car. I sped off running red lights and stop signs. I turned the corner and parked in the parking lot. I jumped out the car, left it running, and told the girls to stay there, that I would be back.

Wanda and Tesha kept saying, "No, we're coming with you!" And Ty said, "Don't go over there unless you have a gun." As they were talking, I got on the phone and called Jason and told him Edward just violated me. I didn't care that they pulled out a gun, I felt disrespected because I was with a bunch of females and they were scared. The girls got out the car and I asked Wanda, "Did you get the keys out the car?"

She was busy on the phone calling everybody telling them what happened, she left the car running. Soon as she went back to the car I ran towards Jason's house. I ran because I didn't want the girls to come with me because I knew it was about to be a shoot out. As I was running through the grass I saw Jermaine, so I started to talk to him as I waited for Jason to come outside. I didn't tell Jermaine what was going on because the less people knew, the better. Jermaine said that he was waiting for his girl, so I sat with him until his girl came.

Jason and his cousin Marvin came shortly thereafter. I started telling Jason and Marvin what happened and then Marvin said, "It seems like I need my hammer." I said, "I thought you were going to bring it." Then I got on my phone. I called Blue and told him that I was coming to get his hammer. As we walked up the path to Blue's building, I see Ty and she said, "Your mother and a whole bunch of people just went to look for Edward."

I asked why Ty wasn't with them and she said, "I didn't want to get shot." I couldn't do anything but laugh. As we were talking, I heard a crowd of people coming from the building where Edward was last seen. So I ran to Blue's building and ran up the steps to the fourth floor.

He saw me running, I guess from his window, because as soon as I got on his floor, he had the gun in his hand. As soon as he passed me the gun, the staircase door opened, and my heart dropped. I thought it was the police, but it was Jason and Marvin. They asked me, "Why did you run?" I said, "I heard all that noise and I didn't want Edward to shoot at anyone."

I told Blue that I was going to hold his hammer down for the night, and we all walked down the steps. We got out the building and didn't see Ty, and then I heard females arguing so we started walking towards the noise. So as we turned the corner we saw a large crowd, mostly females. I saw Ty standing by herself away from the crowd, and then I saw Wanda and Tesha screaming, saying "Come back outside!"

I looked further into the crowd. I even saw my mother screaming. I went to the middle of the crowd and asked, "What happened?" Everybody started screaming at once. Out of all of them screaming, I heard my mother say, "Edward said he shoots bitches, and then he ran up the steps!"

So that just made my blood boil. I went back to where Jason and Marvin were standing and said, "Y'all know what time it is when we see Edward." I looked up at the building and at almost every window, somebody was looking out. That's when Marvin said, "I think that's him, looking out the window on the fifth floor."

Just as I was about to pull the gun out and shoot at the window, Edward walks out the building by himself with no shirt on and heading towards the crowd. My first instinct was to grab my gun because if he were to make any sudden moves, I would have had to shoot him before he shot into the crowd.

So as he got closer to the crowd he started talking, I couldn't hear him clearly. All I remember hearing was one of the females say, "Pop that tough shit now! Don't you shoot bitches!" That's when I started walking towards Edward and I said, "You shoot bitches, right?" Edward started backing up towards the building. I turned around and saw Jason and Marvin walking toward me. So you know we were about to whoop his ass.

Edward started talking and said, "Fight me a fair one." I still don't didn't know if Edward had a gun on him. Before he could say anything else, I swung a left hook, connecting with his mouth. Soon as I pulled my hand back, his mouth started to pour out blood. He still was trying to back up into the building. I took my gun out to hand it to Jason since he was the closest.

Before I could hand it off, out of the corner of my eye, I saw Edward take off into the building. I immediately gave chase. Now I was running with the gun in my hand through the building. Edward ran to the back staircase and up the stairs. I was thinking he was going to be waiting right there with a gun pointed at me soon as I opened the door. I was in the moment and didn't think to stop chasing him. Soon as I opened the door and enter the staircase, I saw Edward. The next thing I knew we were staring into each other's eyes, then it was a loud gunshot, BOOM!

Epilogue

Since completing Barcelona Brownsville: Life in the Hood, I began writing several more books that will be published in the coming years. One such book will be a children's book for my daughter. In the summer of 2012, I became a first time father to a beautiful little girl name Haven. Haven changed my life for all the right reasons. I am working hard so she doesn't ever have to live her life in the hood. She makes me look back on how I turned all these negative situations, into a positive outcome. I went from selling drugs to becoming an employed hard working man. I went from trying to take a person's life, to being a role model in my daughter's life and raising her in a right and healthy way. This is only one of many ways, of how one person can changed their life around, in a short period of time. Just because you are from a low-income and high crime neighborhood, doesn't mean you have to live like you are. Don't give up, and don't give in! Trust me there are a lot of opportunities in this world for us. If you think it's impossible for a positive outcome, just re-read Barcelona Brownsville: Life in the Hood and look at the progress I made, you too can make progress in your own personal life. Thank you for taking the time to read my book!

Life in the Hood Dictionary

5th gun:	forty five caliber semi automatic pisto
Bang with:	hang with
Beat down:	ass whipping
Beef:	an all out war, usually doesn't end until a person is dead
Bid:	a jail term
Blazing:	shooting
Buck 50:	a cut from a razor blade or any sharp object, from ear to mouth usually needing about a hundred and fifty stitches to close
Chirps:	radio, walkie talkie
Clipped:	shot to death
C.O.:	Correctional Officer
D's:	Detectives
Deaded you:	borrowed something but won't give it back
Fiend:	dope fiend, a junkie that can't go without drugs, will do anything to get it
Fronting:	acting tough in front of a crowd of people
Gees:	store on Glenmore Avenue

Barcelona Brownsville: Life in the Hood

Grill: staring at another person while negative thought runs through their minds thoughts of hurting that person

Grip: a handgun

Hold them down: don't let nothing happen

Hood: usually a home for low income people, also known as one's territory

Johnny Pump: fire hydrant, usually the color red

K: short for an AK47, a fully automatic rifle

Let 'em eat: illegal activities, sale of drugs

Macking: hanging around enjoying friends company, relaxing alone or with others

Mad: angry, also means a group of whatever you are referring to

Movie: shoot up a street

Navi: short for Navigator

Nigga(s): greeting for African American people towards each other, means Brother.

PAL: Police Athletic League. A place where kids play sports, get tutored, learn to read and write and play games.

Peeps: short for people

Popo:	short for Police
Quarter Water:	1. a juice for twenty-five containing mostly water, 2. a twenty-five caliber hand gun
Rat:	snitch
Running with you:	playing on the same team
Shitting:	making other people look bad without trying. Ex: Wearing $700 sneakers while another person had on $50 sneakers.
Skelly:	a hood game played with milk tops filled with wax.
Slid:	leaving unnoticed
Smuts:	hoes
Snuff:	punching a person continuously in their face.
Thirsty to be down:	willing to do anything to fit in
Tombs:	jail, Rikers Island
Violate:	embarrassed in front of people
Walkers:	uniform officers that patrol on their feet
Work:	weed, marijuana
WTF:	abbreviation for What The Fuck, usually using in text or internet talk.

About The Author

Alquan Pinkard was born and raised in Brooklyn New York. Alquan spends his time writing children's books and working hard. He is the acqusition Manager of Urban and Street Literature at Pacific Raven Press where he mentors new and young authors.

He tours frequently and gives lectures on street life, gangs, and making positive change, often motivating others to achieve success in their lives while pursuing their dreams.

Alquan Pinkard splits his time between his home in Pennsylvania and his home in Hawai`i, where he enjoys the solitude and tranquility of living a quiet life. Alquan continues to be successful. He spends his time caring for and raising his beautiful daughter Haven.

www.ingramcontent.com/pod-product-compliance
Lightning Source LLC
Chambersburg PA
CBHW050646160426
43194CB00010B/1828